S0-AXV-072

YOUNG ONLY ONCE

Secrets of Fun and Success

by

CLYDE M. NARRAMORE, Ed.D.

Co-author: RUTH E. NARRAMORE

Illustrations by Glenn Davis

ZONDERVAN
PUBLISHING HOUSE

OF THE ZONDERVAN CORPORATION | GRAND RAPIDS, MICHIGAN 49506

YOUNG ONLY ONCE
Copyright 1957 by Clyde M. Narramore
Pasadena, California

Thirty-fifth printing 1979
ISBN 0-310-29972-1

Printed in the United States of America

CONTENTS

ACKNOWLEDGMENTS

A NUMBER OF PEOPLE have cooperated to make *Young Only Once* possible. College and high school students have assisted greatly by meeting with the author to plan the contents of the volume. They have also advised the author throughout the development of the manuscript, and have reviewed the near-finished manuscripts.

Grateful appreciation is also expressed to the following who have made valuable contributions to the book: Mr. Lloyd Ahlem, Mr. Lloyd Hamill, Rev. Loy McGinnis, Mr. Sam Pollach, Mrs. Georgiana Walker, Dr. Donald Robertson, Dr. Clyde W. Taylor and Mr. Benjamin S. Weiss.

Appreciation is expressed to Moody Press for permission to use excerpts from material written by Russell V. DeLong and Harold L. Lundquist, published in the booklet, *Careers*.

Special and loving appreciation is expressed to my wife, Ruth E. Narramore, who has served as co-author.

1

LOTS OF FUN!

BOB AND SHARON were still laughing as the roller coaster squeaked to a standstill.

"Have fun?" shouted the rest of the gang who had watched from a milder vantage point.

"Fun!" exclaimed Sharon, "I'll say! It was terrific. I never screamed so much in my life."

"You can say that again," Bob agreed grinning broadly as he helped Sharon regain a footing on terra firma.

"Wanna go again?" he added, tongue in his cheek.

"Not on your life. Well, not for at least fifteen or twenty minutes anyhow. Give me a chance to recuperate first."

Bob laughed.

"Guess we both need to recuperate," he answered. "My stomach is still churning. Shall we do our recuperating on a hot dog or a ride on something else?"

Bob and Sharon and the whole gang were having fun—lots of fun. They always have fun when they get together.

And it doesn't seem to make much difference whether they are riding on a roller coaster, playing volley ball, having a song fest, or sipping sodas. They have fun doing it — and fun being together. But why shouldn't they? They're *young only once*.

Real honest-to-goodness fun is priceless. It is wholesome and uplifting and makes you a finer person. And it's something that's pleasant to remember. Any kind of fun that doesn't do this is a counterfeit—and it isn't what you're really looking for. No one has more real fun than a Christian. It's the kind that's *right* for you.

One of the secrets of happiness is the ability to have fun. Fun is like a city: It is found in the state of mind and when it is built upon the solid foundation of godliness, it will last a lifetime—your lifetime!

It's Good for You

Fun is a necessity—a pleasing necessity. It's an important ingredient for maintaining good mental health.

It's true that "all work and no play makes Jack a dull boy." God made us that way. He gave us a capacity to enjoy and He expects us to be joyful. God commands us in His Word to *rejoice,* to be *exceeding glad,* and to *be happy* (blessed). Surely we as Christians have more reason to be happy and to have fun than any other people.

Having fun is extremely important from the standpoint of developing your personality. It's hard to be a restricted introvert or a sour-faced pessimist when you are in the throes of active fun. When you're having a good time the whole world looks bright and everyone seems to be your friend. It helps to temper life's disappointments so that when you *do* face them, you do so in a more relaxed and refreshed frame of mind.

God tells us that "a merry heart doeth good like a

10

medicine" (Prov. 17:22). So you see, fun is good for you. Here, for once, is something you not only *need*—but you also *like*.

Action!

Who wants to sit around? Let's get going!

Your life should be thrillingly packed with action. Be a joiner. Be a doer.

Don't hesitate to participate. The right kind of activity — in school, in church, in your community, through sports or clubs or organizations—all these can add up to make you an interesting person. Active participation helps to develop your leadership ability. It helps you to gain self-confidence and poise. And you will cultivate new friendships.

What are some of these activities?

The list is almost endless. Just think about it. There are all kinds of clubs and hobbies and athletics and organizations—and most of them are available to *you*. The scope of interest can be anything from journalism to stone polishing. From Bible study groups to flower arranging. From auto mechanics to ping-pong. There's a hobby or an activity for everyone. So take your choice.

"But I don't *feel* like it. It takes too much effort."

Dull—or lazy? Not necessarily. Young people who react like this may have a health problem. Better check.

It's possible that you just aren't physically up to enjoying life. If you're tired or cross most of the time, it's easy to see that you're not going to have fun. How can you? If this sounds like you, don't placidly continue in your poor-health rut. Use action here, too. See your school physician or family doctor. Eat a proper diet. Exercise. Sleep. You're never too grown-up to need the good, basic common-sense rules of good health. Everyone needs all the wholesome energy God meant him to have. And that means you, too.

The more you *know how* to do, the more fun you

will have, and the more popular you will be. Remember, no person is so uninteresting as the one without interests.

Don't be afraid to try something new. If you're a beginner, admit it—and you'll find plenty of help. And you won't be a beginner long.

So plunge into activity—and do it *with zest.* You'll have the time of your life. And who knows — your hobby, or avocation, could even develop into your vocation some day. It has happened to many, and it's not an impossibility.

Burt found that out. When he was in high school, he chose printing as a hobby. It was a random selection. It wasn't that printing was his "first love." He was just curious. And he *did* find it quite fascinating. Three years later in college he took an advanced course in printing and graphic arts. He enjoyed it and then forgot all about it. It was just a hobby—a new area of learning. He was having fun!

In another five years Burt was on the mission field. Now for the first time his hobby paid off. He saw the great need of getting the gospel message to the natives in an attractively printed form. So he set up one of the finest printing plants in that section of the world and put his "hobby" to a practical use. Today Burt turns out over a million pieces of Christian literature a year. All from a hobby. Back then he just tried it for fun—but he's glad now that he did.

Can you think of some hobbies or activities that may appeal to you? Perhaps it's art, or music, science, photography, language, gardening, swimming, tennis, homemaking, crafts, woodwork, journalism, stamp collecting—and, well, you name it! With all those to choose from—don't fail to choose! Hobbies are good for you—and they're fun!

Special Friends

Mark Twain once said, "To get the full value of joy you must have somebody to divide it with."

This is true. That's why one of the best things that can happen to a person is to have a fine Christian friend.

There is a rich and deep reward in sharing things with a friend. You share your fun and your sympathy and your talk. You do things together, go places together.

It is amazing how much one can learn from a friend. It becomes a chain reaction of inspiration and challenge. And there's an extra dividend, too. Learning how to "click" with one person teaches you how to do it with others.

Where can a person meet someone who will be a good friend? It's not hard to do — if you go to the right places. One of the best places is in your church, in organizations like the choir or a gospel team. And of course, Sunday school. And Christian summer camps. And Christian clubs and parties and social gatherings. And youth rallies. And Christian colleges. Wherever there are Christians you'll find a potential chum. So be on the alert.

But there's more to it than just developing a friendship. If you want to *keep* that special friend, you have to treat him right.

Never take him for granted. It's up to you to put more into your friendship than you expect to get out of it. Constantly be on the lookout for ways to help him. A real friend is unselfish and consistent. None of this business of being "gushy" one day and aloof the next. And be loyal. A friend is worth defending.

Learn how to keep secrets. When Dave (or Jane) tells you something in confidence, he wants to know beyond the shadow of a doubt that you will never tell another person.

Sharing spiritual blessings with a special friend can be a real joy — memorizing Scripture together, praying together, witnessing together. And you'll have the privilege of living the kind of life day in and day out that will inspire your friend to become a deeper Christian.

The Gang

There's no substitute for the friendship you have with that "special" person. But doing things with the "gang" is fun, too. And important fun.

Of course, everyone wants to be accepted — *really* included as a part of the gang. The young person who is always on the "edge" instead of in the swirl of things is many times lonesome. And he is missing out too— because the real fun is in the swirl!

But how to get *in?* Try this. Forget about yourself and think of others. Then *do* something. Learn to do it well. Can you imagine the girl or fellow who plays the piano or accordion well being left out of the gang? Of course not!

The gang? Sure. But just be certain it's the *right* one. To be a part of the wrong group can be fatal to your Christian life. Don't forget that a gang by its very nature requires like-mindedness. This means similar interests and desires. Many gangs participate in activities that just aren't meant for Christians. If you're in one like that, you'd better get out—and do it fast. It can only be a bad influence on you. Surround yourself with fine Christian friends with whom you can fellowship. Then you can have the kind of fun that *leaves you feeling good!*

God knows the pitfalls of the wrong gang. There are many Bible verses on this subject. Let's look at Psalm 1. "Blessed is the man that walketh not in the counsel of the ungodly, nor standeth in the way of sinners, nor sitteth in the seat of the scornful."

Doesn't this apply perfectly?

At first it's just a casual *walk* with the ungodly gang. It doesn't sound so bad, but it's insidious. Next you've stopped to *stand* with them. And finally you've settled down to *sit* with them.

So run past sin as fast as you can—and get as far

away from it as you can. Never slow down to a mere walk when sin is around. It happens just the way God describes it. You walk, you stop and you sit. Before you realize it, your so-called fun has turned into sin. And all the joy is gone. It will be like straw in your mouth. Just straw. Tasteless. Empty. Straw.

You don't want counterfeit living. You want *real* life. And real Christian fun!

What to Do?

"It's okay to say we should have fun," grumbled Gerry, "but what is there for a Christian to do? If we don't dance, go to night clubs or shows what's there left?"

"What's left?" exclaimed Joy. "Why everything that's worthwhile—that's what!"

And Joy was right.

Everything that's worthwhile — everything that's wholesome and uplifting — everything that leaves you feeling good afterward—that's the kind of fun there is for a Christian. And there's plenty of it to be found.

People like Gerry who aren't merry because their Christianity "limits" their fun are only revealing their own personal lacks. Lacks? Yes, lacking in spirituality, in personality, in imagination, in versatility, and in Christian training.

What do I mean? Simply this. *He's lacking spiritually* because a person who is in close fellowship with the Lord will have no interest in worldly amusements. In fact, such amusements will be distasteful to him. God tells us to "love not the world, neither the things that are in the world. If any man love the world, the love of the Father is not in him" (1 John 2:15).

He's lacking in personality because a person who is alive and interesting and vital can always think of something to do, and have a good time doing it. It's usually the "drips" who don't know what to do with themselves.

He's lacking in imagination because with all the

15

many, many things there are to do, if he can't think of *something*, oh, brother — he'd better start sharpening up a little. And it doesn't take much to keep plenty busy having lots of fun.

And *he's lacking in versatility* because he just doesn't know *how* to do anything. In that case, he'd better start learning, if he doesn't like being "left out."

And *lacking in Christian training* — because he just doesn't *know*. We don't get our satisfaction through the things we do, but rather, through Christ, and through being in God's will.

The fact is, non-Christians have a harder time finding something to do than Christians do. That's right. Much harder, because they try to find satisfaction in the worldly amusements. And when it's all over, all they have is an empty shell. Empty—and flat. So they look for something else to give them a "kick." But that doesn't satisfy either. And they'll never find what they are looking for until they find Christ!

When I was in my teens, I lived in a small community surrounded by a desert. And I loved it. To me, a desert was the most wonderful place in the world to live. We had picnics, weiner roasts, horseback rides, corn roasts, steak fries, parties, church doings, sports and the like. We would take our guitars along and sing and play games and tell stories until almost—(too late). We had so many exciting things to do that we could never get them all done. It was thrilling! In fact, I often wondered what kids did who *didn't* live on the desert.

Now after having traveled in various parts of the world, I know that fellows and girls can have fun anywhere. Fun is up to the people who are having it. And there's nothing more fun than fun. Christian young people don't need to go to worldly places to have good times. By the way, if you have to argue with the Lord about where you are going, then you are the one who is wrong, because the Lord never is.

And have you ever thought of this: There are some

things that a Christian *can* do that a non-Christian *can't*. You can go to all kinds of church functions, youth rallies, Christian films, Christian parties and take part in gospel teams. This is fun, too.

What to do? Just start thinking. There are many school functions that are suitable for Christians. Too, there are banquets and all kinds of parties. There are song fests, sight-seeing trips, camping excursions, and games that range from checkers to golf. And when it comes to sports, there are swimming, boating, fishing, hiking, horseback riding, bicycle riding, skiing, skating, sledding, tennis, volleyball, basketball, handball, softball, ping-pong—so on and on the list goes. You can't exhaust the possibilities. Chances are, you haven't even started. And yet you're wondering what to do?

Oh, yes, don't forget picnics and other get-togethers. They are easy—a little food, a place, and some people.

Music also offers many good times—from concerts to Christian records. And as Christians, we have a real capacity to enjoy music because we have a song in our hearts.

Just one word of warning: There's *so much to do,* so much fun at your fingertips, that you won't be able to do it all. But it's lots of fun trying!

Funnish But Not Foolish

Having fun is not playing the fool.

We all know those "characters" who love to have fun at someone else's expense. Bud was that kind of guy. One day he was passing down the hallway where Larry was bending over the drinking fountain. Just for a laugh, Bud pushed Larry's head down. Ouch! Larry's teeth struck the fountain. Bud had his fun. Larry lost three front teeth.

I knew a young fellow who was a daredevil. Oh, it was lots of fun. So *he* thought — that is, until one day he foolishly jumped from one speeding car to another. But this time he missed. The result: seriously injured legs. But he was fortunate that he came out alive. The end of the story? Now he's a pitiful sight, going through life with only one leg—never able to run and jump again. And all because he couldn't tell the difference between being funny and being foolish.

Let's be mighty certain our fun really is fun. There's no use doing something that you'll be embarrassed over the rest of your life. Embarrassment is never fun.

Watch your timing, too. Something that is "terrifically" funny at one time or at one place can be completely out of order in another situation. The Bible says, "There is a time to every purpose . . . a time to weep, and a time to laugh . . ." (Eccl. 3:1, 4). So pause a moment to ask yourself if being funny *right now* is appropriate.

And in *all* your fun keep an even keel. Anticipate the other person's reaction. Be considerate. Don't do things that you'll regret. *Funnish,* yes, *but not foolish!*

Right and Wrong

We live in a world of right and wrong, of good and evil, and we have a definite responsibility to distinguish between them. From childhood to old age we must constantly discriminate between the things that are fine and uplifting and those things that are wrong or harmful, or even *just unimportant.*

But most of our non-Christian schools don't accept this. They tell us that a thing is right or wrong according to the way it is accepted by our society and culture —that it's all a matter of viewpoint.

What poison! Don't ever get taken in by it.

This theory is all the more dangerous because it has some truth in it. Yes, there are some things that are relative. But underneath there is a hard and unchangeable core of moral right and wrong. This core is *never* relative. Centuries ago Plato recognized this when he said, "People and things change. Principles and facts — never!"

Society cannot change God's law of right and wrong. Custom will not change it. Time does not change it.

This law is fixed—forever!

Here, then, is one area in which we especially need God's guidance. And His Holy Word is the perfect guide. Constant close fellowship with Christ will give you discernment so that you can see where the line should be drawn. On the other hand, when you are not close to the Lord, you won't be able to distinguish right from wrong. When this happens, you're on shaky territory. You become open prey for Satan, and he will cause you to believe a lie.

Jokes and stories can be lots of fun. A good laugh is a healthy outlet. But wait. Don't laugh or even listen if that story isn't right. It's your place to *ban* anything questionable.

Smoking? Of course not! Because you know tobacco is harmful to your body, and your body is the very dwelling place of the Holy Spirit. Today there is definite, authoritative medical proof that 80 percent of all lung cancer cases would not have occurred if the victim had not been a smoker.

Smoking is also a dirty, obnoxious habit. In short —*it smells!* The odor fills a room or a car, settles in draperies, carpets, upholstery, clothes and hair. And most smokers probably don't realize that it takes days to get it out.

But the smoking habit isn't easily stopped. Some say, "Oh, I could stop if I wanted to." But the truth is, they can't. Not without the help of the Lord. That's how it was with Lieutenant Loeffler, a fellow shipmate of mine in the Navy. We were both anti-aircraft officers.

Loeffler was a tremendous young man—tall, broad-shouldered and swarthy complexioned. A graduate of the University of Michigan, he was unusually talented, and every inch a man.

One day I had the privilege of leading him to the Lord. Then we started having daily Bible studies together. By the end of the first week we were studying the third chapter of First John. Being impressed myself with the first two verses of the chapter, I "waxed eloquent" on them.

A few days later when we were out on the firing line, Loeffler said, "Narramore, have you noticed that I've stopped smoking?"

"Yes, I have. What caused you to stop?"

"It was the third chapter of First John."

"Really? Well, I'm not surprised. Those first two verses are powerful!"

"But it wasn't the first two. It was the *third* verse."

"Third? Well—I don't think I know what the third verse is about."

"It goes like this: 'And every man that has this hope in him purifieth himself, even as He is pure.' When we read that verse the other day, it struck at my heart. All day long I thought about it. I couldn't get it out of my mind. Finally that evening I got by myself and prayed through on the problem. When I got up from my knees I had victory. I threw my two packages of cigarettes away and asked God to take away all desire for tobacco. That was three days ago, and I haven't touched any since."

God *did* give Lieutenant Loeffler complete victory over smoking. But the struggle included more than smoking. I am convinced that it was a battle of surrendering his *all* to Christ. That day marked a turning point in his life.

God was more interested in Loeffler's total dedication than in his cigarettes. But the cigarettes were a part of his surrender. Without forsaking them there was no complete surrender. God doesn't dislike cigarettes, dancing, drinking and other worldliness as much as He does our *refusal to give them up*. You see, such refusal is disobedience and rebellion! And God never gives His best to those who aren't fully surrendered.

Christians don't have to carry around a long list of "do's" and "don'ts." As they surrender to Christ, as they make Him Lord of their lives, He will tell them what to do—and what *not* to do.

Take the case of Irene. She was beautiful, vivacious and likeable. She grew up in a typical American home where Christianity was a theory but not a reality. Here's the way she tells it:

"I was in college when I first understood the claims of Jesus Christ. I could not resist. I opened my mind and heart to His tender, loving call. I do not think I could have done otherwise.

"Until then, there was nothing I enjoyed more than a martini. I smoked quite a little. I *loved* dancing. Right away I instinctively felt it was wrong to smoke and drink. So I stopped. But dancing was different. I loved the music and the friendship and the relaxation.

"My new-found faith led me to study the Bible and to memorize verses. Little by little the Lord began to speak to me about dancing. No one told me it was wrong (although I had begun to suspect it). But the Lord dealt with me secretly, and when He did, I stopped dancing.

"Now as I look back, I know why it was wrong. It took me away from Christian friends and Christ-centered activities. It led me into an environment that could not possibly help me to grow closer to Christ. Undoubtedly I was a stumbling block to both the saved and the unsaved. Summing it up, it broke my fellowship with the Lord."

So, like Irene, study the Word. Then in a secret, wonderful way it will challenge and cleanse you.

What girl or fellow wants the second-best in a husband or wife because bad habits have spoiled the chances to marry a really clean Christian person? Bad habits aren't fun! They are chains—*heavy* chains.

Yours for the Taking

There's nothing more wholesome than clean fun.

Occasionally I meet a young person who is apparently afraid to let his hair down and enjoy life, *really* enjoy it. Somewhere in the back of his mind there seems to linger a fear that fun for young people is not right.

But don't you believe it. Not at all! Clean, wholesome fun is an honor to our Savior.

It makes you feel good afterward. True, many young people unfortunately indulge in what is often called fun but might better be labeled with the old fashioned (and truthful) word, *sin*. Never mistake sin for fun. Your yardstick should be: Is this activity honoring to the Lord; do I really feel good afterward? God tells us, "Whether therefore ye eat or drink, or whatsoever ye do, do all to the glory of God" (1 Cor. 10:31). So you see, it's really God's yardstick. And it's up to us to use it.

Once you have this yardstick in hand, fun is yours for the taking. So go after it, and you'll find happy times that will leave happy memories.

Lots of fun! Why not? You're *young only once!*

2

THAT PERSON CALLED YOU

How MUCH do you know about that person called *you?* Oh, yes, I know, you have the usual number of hands, your toes wiggle—but how about *you?*

One of a Kind

You are wonderfully unique. Different. There never has been and never will be another person *exactly* like you. Even "identical" twins aren't precisely identical. You are a blend of your heredity and your environment: a fascinating God-mixed combination of traits and talents, attitudes and abilities. To be *you* is an exciting experience. *You* are the only one who will ever know what it is like.

Not Perfect!

Good looking — just average — or even homely. It makes little difference when personality is involved. Because personality is much more dominant than looks.

I have known people (and I'm sure you have, too) who were unattractive as far as their looks were concerned—but they had charming personalities. The fellow or girl who relies too heavily on good looks to gain popularity is building on a wrong premise—and is in for a *big* let down. There's no substitute for an appealing personality. It's one of the most important ingredients of success.

So if you're not pretty or handsome, just remember that people with defects or handicaps can often develop such winning personalities that other folks scarcely even notice these deficiencies.

I think of a young fellow named Casey. He was much shorter than average — and slight. "Pint-size," they called him. When he first started his job, he looked extremely insignificant beside the other fellows in the office who all towered above him. However, he was well-trained and capable—and he was determined to succeed! A consistent, happy disposition, good common sense and a ready smile added up to give him a good start. He was quietly friendly and genuinely interested in everyone he met. Soon his fellow-workers were saying, "That fellow Casey is all right!"

History is full of men who would not allow a handicap to become a liability. Abraham Lincoln was a homely person. Thomas Edison flunked out in school. And Demosthenes had a pronounced impediment of speech. But these disadvantages did not prevent them from making their mark as great men.

In fact, many people who are "a bit too this" or "not enough that" work diligently to compensate for these lacks, and in so doing they develop unusually fine character traits which contribute real strength to their personalities. And of course, character and personality are much more important than looks.

Does a Christian Need It?

I remember a girl who came to me one day.

"Dr. Narramore," she said, "what do you think about Christians trying to improve their personalities? Do Christians need to worry about such things? I thought all that was automatically taken care of when Christ came into one's life."

The fact is, she was *partly* right. But not completely.

True, God tells us in Colossians 2:10, "Ye are complete in Him [Christ]." This is the ultimate. When Christ takes possession of our lives, He supplies our needs. And when we follow the teachings in the Bible we have the best possible guide for attaining a good personality.

But Christians realize that the Bible is not primarily a book on personality. And a good personality is a *necessity,* not only for your own welfare but for your Christian testimony as well. That is why it is especially important for us as Christians to be at our best.

This doesn't just happen. It requires work. And there are two basic ways that you can improve your personality.

1. Evaluate your strengths and weaknesses. Then consciously work on the weak spots in your personality until they are developed into strengths.

2. Let God take complete charge of your life. God is perfection—and He will perfect you as you let Him take control. No one has a better personality than the Christian who radiates the love of Jesus.

You Showing Through

But just what is this thing called *personality?*

It's you! Yes, *you* showing through—the *you* people learn to know and like—or even dislike. And it's the part of you that makes an impression on other people.

Everyone has heard about a *magnetic* personality; the personality that *attracts* people. What makes a personality magnetic? Simply this. It's the natural outgrowth of a positive outlook; it comes from being cheerful, alert, confident and interesting. All this backed up by dependability, thoughtfulness, kindness and honesty. Try it!

One thing is certain. No one can expect to have a vibrant, attractive personality if he excuses himself by saying, "I'm shy," and then stays quietly within himself, or if he's a big *show-off* trying to impress everyone with his "superiority." So face up to your faults, and then really work on them. If you mean business, with God's help you can overcome them.

"I suppose that's right," you may agree. "But what does a person do when he feels terribly inadequate?"

Cheer up! There's a real cure for an "inferiority complex." Ask George; he should know. Year after year he stayed quietly in the background. He was afraid of new situations. Afraid he would say the wrong thing. Afraid someone would laugh at him. Afraid he wouldn't be accepted. A reticent, insecure individual.

Then one Sunday evening George sat in church and heard a successful young businessman give his testimony of how God had helped him overcome a serious

personality problem. Although George was already a Christian, for the first time in his life he began to realize that God's promises were for him as well as for others. Through Christ he too could have strength and guidance, help and wisdom for each new day. He need not be a "second rate" individual—he was on the winning side. As the speaker ended his testimony, he quoted Philippians 4:13, "I can do all things through Christ which strengtheneth me." George felt like jumping up and shouting. *That's it!* he thought.

26

And it was.

The person who truly believes that God is constantly walking by his side is a confident individual—and he doesn't get easily discouraged.

So accept God's strength for *your* life. He is anxious to help you. When you rely on Him, you can cultivate habits and attitudes that will attract other people to you—and to the Savior you represent. Follow these few basic principles and your popularity should increase!

1. Be sincere. You don't fool anyone when you "fake."
2. Be friendly to *everyone*. The way to have friends is to be one.
3. Be interested in people—but never *nosy*.
4. Be considerate, thoughtful—and don't overlook good manners.
5. Smile a lot—and "bubble" over a little.
6. Be appreciative of others. Remember, everyone likes compliments.
7. Be alert and alive. Don't be afraid to be enthusiastic.
8. Be optimistic. There's no substitute for cheerfulness.
9. Don't always be the hero in your own story. People don't go for conceit.
10. Be consistent—not given to "moods."
11. Be appropriate. Know what's suitable and act accordingly.
12. Keep your chin up and don't be afraid. Remember, when God is on your side, you can't lose.

Winning Your Way

People, people, people! You can't get away from them—they're on the bus, in the street, at the office, at school, at home. They're everywhere.

God knows this. That's why He tells us in His Word

that "none of us liveth to himself, and no man dieth to himself" (Rom. 14:7).

Since life is made up of living with people, it's important that you learn how to get along with them. Think about it. How do you feel about the people around you? Are you interested? Bored? Friendly? Annoyed? Whatever your feelings may be toward them — the people in your life are extremely important. *Your success and happiness depend on them!* So don't overlook their actions and attitudes concerning *you.*

And what is it that determines how people act and feel toward you?

The answer is simple. It's your own attitude. Yes, *your attitude toward others will determine how they will react toward you.* Think of some people you know and it will be easy to see the truth of this statement.

Take Janet, for example. She is unduly critical. No one in her crowd is safe from being "ripped-apart" by her cutting remarks. Everything she says belittles someone, or something. Result—people avoid Janet.

But Bruce wears a friendly smile and has a hearty "Hi!" for everyone on the campus. And he's not afraid to speak a good word for his friends. When help is needed, he's right on the spot ready to give a hand. Result — (you've guessed it) Bruce is popular, has more friends than he can count.

That's how it works. It always does!

Can you remember some of your own experiences— the morning you came to breakfast grumpy, touchy and half-angry? No one at the table spoke pleasantly to you, did he? And you thought the whole family had it in for you.

And then there was the time you and old Professor Fink got caught in the rain. You laughed with him at your predicament and had a friendly talk together. Strange how interesting he was. Come to think about it, you'd never spoken to him before!

As you think back on your day by day contacts, you can clearly see what effect your attitude has had on the people in your life. It's almost as simple as:

Your anger = an angry reaction.
Your friendliness = friendliness in return.
Your sarcasm = a bitter retort.
Your smile = a smile in return.

Does your attitude toward people need improving? If so, don't wait! Ask God to give you strength, wisdom and patience — and then conscientiously try to apply the principles that will help you in getting along with people. It's not easy, but worth every effort you can muster. And what will happen? The first thing you know, you'll develop a truly desirable personality. And you'll gain many friends.

A Likeable You

What makes a person likeable? It's not hard to describe the attributes of a truly likeable person. Think of your best friends. Cheerful — generous — tactful— tolerant — interesting — dependable — honest — sincere — energetic — helpful — happy — ready with a compliment — slow to criticize. See the picture? Does it look like you?

This personality inventory may help you evaluate your likeability. Read each question, then mark your answer "yes" or "no." It will really challenge you. So let's go:

1. Are you reasonably free from selfishness? Yes No
2. Are you a good loser in a game? Yes No
3. Can you take criticism without showing resentment? Yes No
4. Are you kind and generous in judging people and their actions? Yes No
5. Are you thoughtful and considerate of others? Yes No
6. Do you respect the opinions and rights of others? Yes No
7. Do you listen attentively when others speak to you? Yes No

8. Are you given to complimenting? Yes No
9. Do you believe God is interested in your every day life? Yes No
10. Do you try to practice Christ's command to "love others as thyself?" Yes No
11. Do you speak distinctly and in a pleasant voice? Yes No
12. Do you generally use good English? Yes No
13. Do you refrain from correcting the mistakes of others? Yes No
14. Do you avoid saying things that would embarrass anyone who might be listening? Yes No
15. Are you careful not to exaggerate? Yes No
16. Do you refrain from being gossipy? Yes No
17. Do you refrain from envying others? Yes No
18. Do you make and hold friends easily? Yes No
19. Do you lend things to others readily? Yes No
20. Do you pray every day that God will make you more "Christlike"? Yes No

What is your score? The more "yes" answers you have, the more *likeable* you are. If your score is 16 to 20, you're wonderful to know, a worth-while friend. If your score is from 12 to 16, rate yourself as average. That indicates that you're fairly well liked. A score of 8 to 12 is not so good—and below 8, well, you're in a bad way.

Your score is interesting, but even more than that, it can be a valuable guide to help you improve your own likeability. Whatever your score (high or low) better work to change every negative answer to a "yes."

But how? These ideas may help you.

—Make a list of all the unlikeable traits you'd like to eliminate.

—Start today by taking every opportunity to act in the direction of your new goal.

—Earnestly pray about your shortcomings.

—At the close of each day, check yourself for improvements.

30

If you follow these few simple suggestions, you will develop a more likeable personality.

Show Yourself Friendly

Sometimes a person is liked—even admired, but does not make friends easily. The student body president of a Texas school once said, "The difference between being liked and being popular is in a person's reaction to others. The popular people know just what to do or say in most situations. More than that, they are very friendly and openly interested in everybody."

The formula for making friends hasn't changed in thousands of years. Solomon took his scroll and wrote, "A man that hath friends must show himself friendly" (Prov. 18:24). And twentieth century psychologists haven't been able to improve on this God-given way to friendship.

If you find yourself alone, watching people from your corner, chances are you haven't shown yourself friendly. Now be honest with yourself. Have you? Mike sums it up when he says, "There're not many of us who can resist a cheerful smile and a friendly 'Hello.' "

Your Friends

Just whom do you want for a friend?

Cicero claimed that "a friend is, as it were, a second self." If this is true, the people you choose for friends are exceedingly important.

Christian young people have the most fun with Christian friends. They share the same ideals, the same goals. It's easy for them to agree on where to go—what to do—and how to do it. The Bible puts it this way: "Can two walk together, except they be agreed?" (Amos 3:3). That's the true basis of friendship.

Ron and Dick became friends when they tied for second place at a swimming meet. But soon they found that they had a lot more in common than just swimming. Ron is a Christian Endeavor leader; Dick is the

31

program chairman in his church youth group. These fellows enjoy swimming together. But more than that, they enjoy sharing plans for their church organizations. They share their hopes, their dreams and their problems. They share their spiritual blessings and their spiritual needs—and they pray together. Such a friendship is a vital one. It has real meaning.

But unfortunately, not everyone is a Christian. So more than likely some of your friends may be non-Christians. Interesting people—many times, fine people. Just what is *your* responsibility to a friend who does not know Christ? You *do* have a responsibility, you know. Your actions, your words, your whole manner of living should be a witness to the fact that you know Christ as your personal Savior and Lord.

Some young people may think that they can give forth a Christian testimony by going in with the worldly crowd. Perhaps they mean well. Their motives may be all right. But there's danger ahead!

Danger like this: A small boy had a cage full of sparrows. He felt quite certain that they could learn to sing like canaries. Why not? So he bought a canary and put it into the cage with the sparrows. "Teach them to sing," he commanded the yellow songster. A couple of weeks later the boy came running to his mother. "Mom," he cried, "the canary is chirping like the sparrows!"

So watch your step! You can never pull someone out of a deep pit by getting in there yourself. And that's the way it is with a Christian. When we become like the world, we lose our power to influence people for Christ. This does not mean we should never have any non-Christian friends. But it does mean we should live an out-and-out Christian life in any situation. And never compromise convictions. They are priceless.

It's a challenging command which Christ has given us, that of presenting the Gospel to the world. But when we remember that we're *"in* the world, but not *of* the world," we can do it without sacrificing our loyalty to Him!

Friendship Know-How

Is there someone you don't like? Someone who just "irks" you or "gets under your skin?" The temptation is to ignore him, but being rude is definitely *not* the answer. If you are closely associated with someone who doesn't appeal to you, do something about it. It might surprise you—and work.

1. Try to understand what has made him the way he is.
2. Look for his good qualities. Everyone has some.
3. Always be courteous. People respond to courtesy.
4. Be gracious. Christ's way is to "love your enemy."
5. Ask the Lord to give you a good attitude. Pray for him.

If you really want someone to change his mind about something, don't argue. It's definitely the wrong approach. No one likes to lose an argument—so don't start one and don't continue one that someone else has started. Instead, try encouraging the other fellow to tell you his ideas. And while he talks, listen to him. Don't interrupt. Don't contradict. Just listen.

Be sure you understand what he means—and if you disagree, tell him so (if you think it's necessary)—but do it in a friendly manner. By all means, don't start telling him with just any words. There's no excuse for bluntness. So use some diplomacy. Start with, "I may be wrong, but . . ." or "Maybe you're right, but . . ." Don't forget these words. If you can say them and mean them, they'll work wonders. It's almost like magic.

Another secret of having and keeping friends is to be quiet about their faults. Everyone has them and everyone makes mistakes. But talking about them seldom helps. So be slow to criticize. It will pay off. People won't criticize you so fast, either.

On the other hand, people like to be admired. So be sincerely generous with your praise. Take the trouble to notice the things people do well and tell them about it. They like praise, and when you give it, they'll like you, too.

It's Up to You

So now you see yourself. *You*. The only person who ever has or ever will have your exact potential.

God has given you the basics—but it's up to you to make the most of them. Don't be satisfied with a second-rate personality. You *can do* something about it. When you have a pleasing personality, you will not only enjoy life more yourself, but others will enjoy it more, too—because of knowing you. And a Christian with a winning way can use that attribute to win others for Christ.

So be your best. You can have a charming personality: friendly, alert, helpful, kind, confident, poised, ambitious! Be unafraid ". . . strong in the Lord, and in the power of his might."

And be your best for God!

3

A LOOK AT YOURSELF

PROFESSOR JOHNSON was a grand guy. His classes were always bulging with students. He was popular.

What was he like? Well, after you got past his hearty laugh, dynamic voice, well-pressed suit and his exemplary Christian life, you saw the man.

What did he look like? Uneven, heavy features. Big ears. A large wart on the side of his nose. By any standard he was homely.

Once I heard him laughingly refer to his looks. "Years ago," he chuckled, "I looked in the mirror and said to myself, 'If looks really count, Johnson, you're through right now!' but I liked people so well that I asked God to help me work with them. And believe it or not, He's kept me so busy I haven't had a chance to look in a mirror since."

But during my years on the campus I never heard anyone describe Dr. Johnson as ugly. His honest friendliness, his neat appearance and ready smile combined to make him a fine-looking man.

Just how good looking are *you?*

Wait! Before you look in the mirror make up your mind that you're not going to take what you see too seriously. That mirror is limited. It can't show you all you are or can be. It can only give you an idea of what you have to work with.

Remember, handsome or not, you *can* be good looking!

Of course, an essential part of good looks is good grooming. How handsome can anyone expect to be with grimy hands? Or a baggy suit? There are many easy ways you can help yourself look your best.

Soap and Water

Being clean, *really* clean, is the first step in careful grooming. Plenty of water and soap are a *must*. And don't let the water and suds just slosh over you! Since your aim is to wash away worn out skin, as well as the smudges and grime, go after your cleaning job with a wash cloth, a brush and vigor. While you scrub, be glad you're living in the twentieth century. Just think, your great-grandfather sat in a wooden tub and used a metal scraper!

Unfortunately, soap and water won't keep you free from — excuse the word — odor. Everyone perspires every hour of the day. And don't complain—it's your own private air conditioning system. Nearly a quart of liquid is secreted through the sweat glands all over the body in every twenty-four hours. If your day has been full of tension, or if you have been rushing around, your problem is even greater. No wonder then, that every careful person uses a deodorant. It not only protects one from unpleasant odors, but frequently prevents stained clothing. So choose your deodorant and put it to work today.

Hands and Hair

Hands and hair demand special grooming.

"How often should I wash my hair?" some ask.

Each individual has to figure out his own answer. Bill is a mechanic at the airport. Grease and dust are a part of his routine, so he has to lather his crew cut several times a week. But Sue, the girl he is dating, works at the library. Because her hair is dry and her office is clean, she shampoos her curly red hair only once a week. A good guide is to wash your hair whenever it is dirty. But don't be fooled. Hair gets dirty just from being on your head—there's perspiration and such. So don't ignore a shampoo for more than two weeks.

So far, so good! But girls have a special consideration. Now that your hair is "cleaned and curled," *how are you going to arrange it?* Every attractive girl looks in the mirror to see what best suits her face. If you're in doubt, most hair stylists say that droopy, stringy hair hanging down the side of your face makes you look drab and uninteresting. Hair back, up off your face usually gives you a keener, smarter appearance.

The trend? Natural, soft-looking waves usually do the most for you. (And this "natural look" applies to color, too!)

For good hand care nothing equals a hand brush, a nail file and a few minutes each day to use them. Fellows should know that a girl likes a man's hands with nails evenly cut and short, but most of all, clean! Boys have definite ideas, too.

Bob put it this way: "I like a girl who has neat,

feminine-looking hands. No long, blood-red nails, please! They give me the creeps!"

Dress Right

Another law of good grooming says, "Dress right." Dressing right does not mean having lots of expensive clothes. But it does mean using your clothes wisely.

Take Ruth, for example. Although she has a limited budget for her clothing, she skillfully combines skirts, sweaters and blouses in various colorwise combinations. Everything is immaculate, well-pressed and on hangers. The result? A well-dressed, attractive girl.

"Dress right?" Yes, dress to *suit the occasion*. Sport clothes for outings — but dress-up clothes for church. And don't make the mistake that some do. In their effort to be "casual" they really are just plain sloppy.

I know two girls who basically look a great deal alike. But their clothes make the difference. Jean's clothes fit her, but Charlotte's don't. Jean's are "smart," but Charlotte's are "plain-Jane." Cost? No, they spend about the same. Charlotte could look just as attractive if she would do these three things: (1) Buy clothes that are "sharp," (2) make sure that they fit, and (3) look in the mirror to see that they are on straight.

The next time you leave the house be sure the clothes you wear are: suitable — clean — becoming — well-fitted — well-pressed — and color matched. And when you're giving yourself that "once-over," don't forget to look down, too. Because basic to your entire appearance are attractive well-cared-for shoes.

True, clothes don't make the man, but there's no doubt about it: The right clothes do make a man—or woman—look better.

More Than Skin Deep

If you are honestly interested in making a top-notch impression day after day, you'll go more than skin deep.

—Eat a balanced diet.
—Get sufficient sleep. Rest and peace of mind are important, too.
—Get exercise in the fresh air.
—Drink plenty of water.
—Take frequent baths.

Such a program is especially important if your problem is an oily skin, a pimply face, too much weight or a lazy, listless feeling. These good health habits will quickly reveal a more attractive, more energetic you! And as Ralph learned, looking your best will give you a better opportunity to witness to your non-Christian friends.

Straight and Tall

"An out of line car doesn't work well," Bruce says. Neither does an "out of line" body. You can give yourself real aches and pains as well as a grouchy disposition just by slumping around. Too much trouble to straighten up? Not if you want to look your best. The way you sit, the way you stand, will give people important clues about the real you. Remember, good posture makes every fellow look more stalwart and masculine and every girl more graceful and feminine.

Your Smile

Smiles are magic. They can cast a spell that will transform gloom into sunshine.

And the person who wears a smile is displaying something that is radiantly beautiful.

How about *you*? Try sneaking up on yourself unexpectedly and taking a look. Is there sunshine on your face? Or do you have to struggle to muster up an artificial excuse for a smile?

Actually, smiling is easier than frowning. When you smile, you conserve your energy—it requires the use of about thirty-six muscles to smile and about ninety-seven to frown. So frown and work overtime, or smile and shorten your working day! A smile is a girl's most effective cosmetic, and a man's best agent.

The Outward Appearance and the Heart

Day after day a good appearance does make it easier for you to have fun with your crowd; easier to be successful in your work; for, as we read in First Samuel 16:7, ". . . man looketh on the outward appearance."

However, don't miss the rest of the verse. ". . . But the Lord looketh on the *heart*."

This is even *more* important!

How about your heart? How does it look to the Lord?

He has not only commanded "clean hands" but also a "clean heart." God provides daily cleansing through prayer and through the reading of His Word. "If we confess our sins, He is faithful and just to forgive us our sins, and to cleanse us from all unrighteousness" (1 John 1:9). "Wherewithal shall a young man [or a girl] cleanse his way? by taking heed thereto according to thy word" (Ps. 119:9).

No matter how well you look on the outside, if you fail to read God's Word and to pray, you will never be clean *inside*.

And what's more, after a while what you are on the inside will show through.

Take What You Have — and Be Happy

I once knew a girl, Sandra (there are "scads" like her), who could never accept her own looks. Sandra wasn't bad looking, but neither should she have tried to enter a beauty contest.

From the time she was eleven, she cut out pictures of exotic movies stars and pasted them around her room. She thought of herself as this one or that one. And so it went.

But Sandra finally grew up—physically, that is. Yet she never gave up her glamorous roles. Like a pre-adolescent, she still played make-believe. Her hair!

She couldn't accept what God gave her. She wanted to be a torrid redhead. Naturally, everyone around church and school was amused. But interestingly enough, the "red" didn't do for her what she expected. So she dyed it bright yellow. What a combination— black and yellow. Black hair growing out of her eyebrows and yellow out of the top of her head. But that combination didn't last long either. She was getting no place fast. So on and on she went—years of rainbow colors.

What was wrong with Sandra? Color blind? No, she had never learned to accept herself. And of course, neither did anyone else accept her. You see, *people who don't accept themselves, don't get accepted by others.*

You may never be Miss or Mr. Universe—but who cares!

The next time you look in a mirror, I suggest that you have a little personal conversation. "Susie" or "Dick" (or whatever it is), you say to yourself, "I'm not blind. I can see what I look like."

And then make up your mind that you're going to be happy about it.

If you are good looking—well, thank the Lord for being so kind to you, and pray hard that you'll never develop into a conceited "jerk." What good is it to be pretty or handsome if people can't stand to be around you?

Suppose you have a face that "only a mother can love." What then? In the first place, cheer up; it probably isn't nearly as bad as you think. Besides that, there are scores of people with that kind of face who have been loved by many. Other people never even think of them as being homely because they like them.

But you're probably neither a raving beauty nor a scarecrow. Most of us fit into that "in-between" category.

The realistic thing to do, no matter what your natural endowments may be—or may *not* be—is to *make the best of what you have.* Dress becomingly and smartly. Comb your hair in an attractive style. Make sure you are always neat and clean. Do the best you can *for* yourself, but not *to* yourself. The person who is overdone looks ridiculous.

After you do all you can to look your best, then forget about it and concentrate on a good personality. When you learn to accept yourself and not try to be someone else, you can be the most likeable person in the world.

And you will be *charming,* too!

4

SMARTER AND SMOOTHER

"I'm thoughtful," or—
     "I'm really quite selfish," or—
          "I get along well with people."

YOUR ACTIONS are speaking! They are loudly announcing the kind of person you are. And whether or not you want it that way, people are listening to what they say! As they listen, they learn all about you—your attitudes, your traits, your manners, and just what code of etiquette you live by.

"Etiquette?" Pete asks with a big question mark. "Who needs a bunch of rules? I get along just fine by using common sense."

Janice feels much the same way: "If you're thoughtful and kind, manners take care of themselves!"

Pete and Janice are sincere, but they are over-simplifying the matter of etiquette. Although kindness and common sense do form the basis for good manners, they do not give all the answers for every social situation. There are many times when you should know the forms and procedures which tradition has established as proper. These forms must be *learned*. And, of course, you want to act acceptably in any group of people at any time, anywhere. This is doubly important for you because a Christian who is well poised and at ease becomes a good representative for Christ.

It is not hard to master the "do's" and "don'ts" of proper etiquette! With a little practice these rules will become so automatic that you won't need to give them a second thought.

Meeting People

Everyone likes a new friend, or a new interest; so meeting people should be fun. And it usually is — if the introduction goes smoothly. Introductions can be absolutely painless when you follow the rules. And it's really quite simple if you always present the man to the woman.

"Miss Martin, may I present Mr. Roberts . . . Miss Martin . . ."

Present the boy to the girl.

"Ruth, may I present Dave Jones . . . Ruth Davis . . ."

Present the younger person to the older person.

"Mr. Hedrick, may I present Sally Clark . . . Mr. Hedrick . . ."

Your response to an introduction is important. A simple "How do you do," a good firm handshake, and a pleasant smile as you look at the person you are meeting, is the proper way to receive an introduction.

Men usually shake hands with each other when they meet for the first time. A girl may or may not wish to shake hands with a man; it's not necessary, just a friendly gesture. A fellow always stands when being introduced to a lady. A girl rises when she is being introduced to an older woman, but she remains seated when a boy or another girl is being introduced to her. Both fellows and girls should shake hands with parents or an older person if it is convenient to do so. (Of course, no gloves.)

What if you are introduced to someone whom you think you have met before? Don't say, "I've known him for years!" or "Why, I've met you before." (Especially if he hasn't the slightest flicker of recognition on his face.) Instead, wait awhile, and then discuss the mystery of where and when. It will save embarrassment.

At the Table

Soup or salad, pie or cake—you automatically reach for a fork or spoon, and in a matter of minutes the food is gone! But how did you eat it? Did you gulp? Did you hunch over your plate? Did you hold your silverware properly?

Your eating manners may be automatic, but they do demand your careful inspection. How do you look when you eat? No one enjoys eating with a friend who is rude.

For instance, getting seated doesn't seem like much of a problem — but there are a few things you must watch. Boys and men, even at an informal table, will take the opportunity to pull back the chair for a girl or lady. (A thoughtful lady makes it easy to do.) Men do not seat themselves until all the women are seated. Then all the guests open their napkins halfway and place them on their laps. After the blessing is asked, the meal is ready to begin.

Does a full array of silver confuse you? Just remember to start with the tools which are set farthest from your plate, and as the meal progresses, work in. If you are in doubt, observe your hostess. You really should wait for her to start each course anyway!

If you should have an accident, such as dropping your spoon or tipping over a glass of water, be calm. Your hostess will come to your rescue.

You might check yourself on these table manners:

> When eating soup, lift your spoon toward the outside edge of the bowl. Quiet please — no sipping noises!
>
> Food is always served from the left.
>
> In America bread is not used to wipe the plate.
>
> A spoon is never left in a cup.
>
> Talk at the table should be pleasant. No accidents, no operations, no tales of horror!
>
> Observe the accepted way to hold silver. How do you hold yours?
>
> No elbows on the table while eating.
>
> If you are always finished eating first—slow down.
>
> If you are always last—speed up!

These rules hold true wherever you eat. When you order at a restaurant, feel free to ask the waiter about words on the menu that you may not understand.

Good table manners are just as easy to make into habits as bad ones: So use *good* manners, and they will soon be habits.

In Public Places

Did you ever say, "No one here knows me; it doesn't matter how I act"?

But don't fool yourself. Even strangers judge you by the things you do. Your manners speak for you in public just as much as they do when you are in the privacy of someone's home. The person who continues an embarrassingly personal conversation in a crowded elevator announces he is not thoughtful. Or if he wears unsuitable clothing on the street, he is showing the world he is without personal pride. Being a public show-off by shouting, laughing loudly and yelling is not only bad manners, but it tells everyone you are immodest and inconsiderate of others.

When you appear in public, you reveal your poise and maturity. On a crowded sidewalk people usually move in two lanes of traffic. Make certain that you aren't the only one going "uptown" in the "downtown" lane! And never stand in front of a doorway! It's not safe for you, and certainly not handy for the door-user.

Church Time

How about your manners in church? Perhaps you haven't given them much thought. The most important thing is to be quiet and reverent. Of course, you should look pleasant and pleased when you see your friends; but in church, the attitude of friendliness bows to the greater one of worship. Your attitude of worship will become meaningful to you as you listen and participate in the service with heartfelt attention.

Even a whisper in church is too much talking, unless that whisper is absolutely necessary. If you see a friend across the aisle, resist that impulse to wave or speak. Give your recognition with your eyes or with a slight flicker of a smile. Church is a place where we meet God. And if your pal should come in and sit next to you and your guest, introductions must wait until later.

But church is not over the minute the last "Amen" is said. Definite greetings, introductions, visiting—all these should wait until you are in the vestibule, or outside of the church. The vestibule is also the place to briefly express your appreciative greetings to the minister.

What to wear? This will be governed to some extent by the customs of dress in your own church group. Sunday best or casual, you must be neatly dressed and carefully groomed. For the fellows, church automatically means a coat and tie. And remember, gum chewing is "out" in church.

When you attend church with your date—the girl

47

walks quietly down the aisle with the fellow and precedes him into a convenient seat of her choice, or if there is an usher, the seat is chosen for them.

Your church etiquette will be no problem when you observe God's standard for worship: "The Lord is in His holy temple: let all the earth keep silence before Him" (Hab. 2:20).

Family Manners

Someone has said, "Manners begin at home."

Your parents were the ones who taught you to hold a spoon—and to say "please!" And just as surely as home is the beginning place for etiquette, it is the natural place to practice good manners so that they become a sincere part of you.

Learning tact with your family will help you get along tactfully with your crowd. Friendly co-operation at home will help you develop into the kind of person who can work well with others. So make the most of these opportunities. Are you thoughtful about things like these:

—Compliment rather than criticize your kid brother (or sister).

—Be fair about time spent on the telephone; someone may be waiting.

—Listen with consideration and sincere interest when an elderly relative talks to you.

—Watch your manners at the table.

—Don't monopolize the bathroom.

All of these situations, and many others, supply you with innumerable opportunities to put good manners to work.

The next time you walk in the front door, don't shed all your kindness and consideration as though you were removing a coat. What kind of person are you at home? That is the *real* you.

The members of your family are the ones you love. So why not let your manners tell them so?

Telephone Etiquette

The next time the phone rings, it may be for you!

So let's do a little checking into telephone etiquette. Acceptable telephone manners are not too different from good manners any time. You see, how you say it is almost as important as what you say. And courtesy is a necessary quality that must be communicated along *with* your words.

"Hello" is the usual way to answer when one receives a personal phone call. However,, when you are answering a business phone, your employer will tell you what he wishes you to say, such as "Dr. Jones' office," or "Gleason's Hardware."

In business it is standard procedure to say, "Who is calling, please?" At home, however, this direct question is too abrupt. If the person being called is not at home, the one answering should ask, "May I take a message?" or "May I tell him who is calling?" It is good manners for the one who has placed the call to leave his name.

The person who makes the call usually suggests the "good-by." But you may, with suitable apologies, terminate the conversation if you need to. Always remember to say, "Thank you for the call." Sometime you may be called to the phone when it is definitely inconvenient. What then? Just politely ask, "May I call you back in a few minutes?" (or in an hour — or tomorrow). But then be sure you *do* call back.

When you are on the phone, your voice is all that represents you. Make it do a good job. You will put your "best voice" forward if you follow these few simple suggestions:

—Don't talk too fast.
—Enunciate clearly.
—Emphasize important words. (Inflection creates interest—monotones bore.)
—Control your volume. Not too loud. Not too soft.
—Don't talk too long.

And by all means, if you are on a party line, take pity on the other party. Give him a "break," too. It's only fair—and it's the Christian thing to do.

Invitations and Parties

Having a party? How do you invite everyone?

Inviting friends by telephone is one acceptable way. Just be sure to remember all the "when's" and "where's" when you talk. And if the person you are inviting can't say a definite "yes" or "no" when you call, it's proper to ask him to call back later and give you his answer.

Is it to be a *special* party? Perhaps then you would rather mail the invitations. They can be either formal or informal, whatever the occasion demands. If you include your telephone number, and "R.S.V.P." (French for *Repondez s'il vous plait*), or the English "Please Reply," it will give you an estimate as to how many to plan for.

When you have the fun of receiving an invitation, reply promptly. Call the party-giver and happily accept or graciously decline the invitation. Then when the special occasion arrives, go expecting to have a good time. Enter wholeheartedly into whatever fun has been planned. It is your responsibility; you know, to help make the party a success. And don't forget to tell your hostess how much you enjoyed yourself.

The engraved (or handsomely printed) invitation is proper for weddings or other formal affairs. An invitation to a church ceremony does not require an answer, but you *are* expected to acknowledge an invitation to a wedding reception or wedding breakfast.

By Mail

Just what kind of letters do you write? Interesting? Inspiring? Suitable? Fun to receive? Or dull?

After all, a letter should be a small picture of yourself, your life, your Chistian testimony and the things you do. At times, it can be a mirror to show your feelings. So when you write again, see if you are really putting some of yourself into the words.

Friendly Letters

Just how should a letter look? If you have forgotten, check some letter forms. Be sure to include the date and your address in the heading. "Dear" is the most widely used, and generally the most suitable salutation.

Don't ever write anything in your letter that might be misunderstood or that you would hesitate to have other people read. As a Christian, your letters should be a real spiritual blessing to those who receive them.

Letters that just "ramble on" are in poor taste.

Thank You Notes

Be prompt! Saying "thank you" by writing a note expresses your appreciation for a gift or for hospitality.

The Bible tells us, "Be ye thankful" (Col. 3:15). But it's also our responsibility to *express* our thanks.

A Sympathy Note

Short and sincere are the requirements when writing a note of condolence. Volumes of words are no more comforting than a sincere thought that is briefly stated.

Nothing can cheer the heart more than God's precious Word. People are also comforted to know that you are praying for them.

Business Letters

Every business letter should be typed and it should follow a definite business form. By all means, be sure every spelling is correct. Your signature is always written by hand.

Travel Time

Suitcase packed? Ticket in your wallet? Then grab a timetable and get on your way. But don't forget your travel manners!

Whether you are a seasoned traveler or not, you should use courtesy, tact and common sense.

Travel etiquette requires that you have a pleasant dignity; that you be poised, but not snobbish; reserved, but not stiff. Occasionally you may talk to other fellow travelers, but in most situations your conversation should be impersonal. Talk about the scenery, the weather, the world situation, but not about yourself, except as you give your personal testimony as to what Christ means to you.

A gentleman does not embarrass a girl who is traveling by inviting her to eat with him, or by asking her to accept any other favors. Proper traveling manners say that just isn't done. It's a good idea to take a magazine, a newspaper or your Bible with you when you go to a dining car or restaurant alone, because you will not want to sit and watch others eat or listen to their conversations. When you are seated at a table with a stranger, it is up to the lady to begin a conversation if she wishes. This is perfectly proper if it is kept impersonal and friendly.

Some of the definite "do's" and "don'ts" of your trip will depend on how you decide to travel. Are you going by plane, train, ship or bus? Just inquire from your local travel agent and he will be glad to give you accurate information about tickets, reservations and procedures.

However you travel, enjoy your trip. If you miss connections, or if something goes wrong, don't forget that "all things work together for good to them that love God, to them who are the called according to His purpose" (Rom. 8:28). Don't expect things to be "just like home." Have a sense of humor. It's the unexpected that helps to make things interesting.

So look around and see what you are passing. Then you'll have a lot to remember later!

Tips on Tipping

Whether you are traveling around the world, or just eating in that little restaurant on the corner, it helps to know a few guides for tipping.

In restaurants: When people are seated at a table, the usual tip is from ten to fifteen percent of the total check. If you are drinking a coke or eating a sandwich at the counter, watch others for your cue. Counter tipping varies: It may not be required.

While traveling: At a train station a porter or "redcap" is on hand to help with one's baggage. How much does he expect? Twenty-five cents a bag is customary, and a small extra tip is sometimes added. On a pullman train the traveler is usually expected to tip the car porter who has made his berth and answered his calls. This tip is usually fifty cents for each day he has been on the train.

If you travel by bus, the driver will help you with your baggage, but he will not expect a tip. On the plane the stewardess will be helpful in many ways, but a tip is never offered. Ship tipping is rather complicated, and depends on the size of the ship and the length of the voyage, so check with your travel agency for definite instructions before you sail.

Everywhere — All the Time

And so it goes. As you work, as you play; as you walk or as you drive, good manners pave the way for successful human relationships.

Don't under-rate the things that your manners tell about you. Good manners say:

"You are a choice friend."

"You are a good worker."

"You are a delightful guest at the party."

"You are poised and self-confident."

Remember, wherever you are, whatever you do, your manners are making you—smarter and smoother!

5

HOW TO SAY IT

It takes more than good looks to make a good impression. People look—and then they *listen!*

Perhaps it's happened to you. Maybe it was at the drug store, or down at the malt shop where you saw her. She was tall and slender with sparkling brown eyes. Her shiny hair was swept back into soft curls. Ah! Here was a real beauty.

Suddenly she spoke — and what a let down! Her loveliness — it was gone, shattered by her harsh, rasping voice.

It's true. A shrill unpleasant voice can ruin an otherwise good first impression. On the other hand, a good voice will make people stop—listen—and want to hear more.

Wait a minute. Do I hear you talking? How do *you* sound?

There are several different ways that you can evaluate your voice—and with reasonable accuracy. If you want to find out how well you are using it, try this:

Cup your hands behind your ears, push each ear slightly forward; then start speaking out loud. Now you hear yourself as others hear you.

Better yet, record your voice and then listen as you play it back. And don't be afraid to be critical!

Too harsh? Too soft? What are you doing with the final sound of each word? Are you talking too fast? Does your voice suggest mental alertness? Or laziness? Listen carefully because you *can* change your voice and the way that you use it.

If you don't like the way you sound, take a cue from Bob. Today he is a speaker for one of the gospel teams sent out by his young people's group. But only two years ago he wasn't even asked to make the announcements for their meetings!

"Your voice is too dull, Bob. Almost a monotone," kindly explained the leader of the group.

Bob was disappointed and almost angry. But he was smart. "I'll show him," Bob vowed. And he began right away to do something about it. He practiced speaking with a wide variation of tones and expression. He experimented by using famous lines and quotations.

"Stop in the name of the law!" he commanded when he turned off the shower. He figured out twenty-five ways to say "Give me liberty or give me death!"

And he also used Scripture. As Bob drove back and forth to school, his car was his audience. It was always a good listener. Bob memorized the first Psalm, the twenty-third Psalm and many other portions of Scripture. He said them over and over again. Not only was Bob improving his speaking but he was learning God's Word at the same time.

A few months later Bob made his comeback. The

leader and the group were surprised with the improvement in Bob's once dull voice.

A different voice? Yes—it *can* be done. Bob did it. And *you* can, too.

So if you're not pleased with your voice, get busy. It's the easiest thing in the world to correct. And you can "do it yourself." Here are a few basic rules to guide you:

—Slow down, give each word a chance.
—Sharpen your pronunciation. Don't drop final "t's" and "d's."
—Avoid a monotone. Vary your tone and pace.
   Speak some phrases high
      —Others low:
   Speak some phrases fast
      —Others slow.
—Don't be a mumbler. Move your tongue, lips and jaws so that you can form each word accurately.
—Relax. Tense vocal chords produce shrill rasping tones.
—Read out loud. It will help you develop clarity of speech, and make you a better reader, too.

Observe these rules, and your voice has a good chance to be at its best. But don't expect it to sound like Sam's or Sally's. It will be distinctly *yours*. And as much a part of the impression you make, as the way you look or the way you act.

So remember, people are listening.

The Words You Use

Words are tools of speech. That's why it is so important to know how to use them. If you've ever read the story *Through the Looking Glass* you'll probably recall that mixed-up character, Humpty-Dumpty, who said to Alice, "When I use a word it means just what I choose it to mean, neither more nor less!"

Hold it! You can't do that. Such use of vocabulary won't work because words do have quite exact mean-

56

ings. If you want *what you say* to be *what you mean,* then it pays to know the right word.

Adjectives are fun to use. Just so they're not abused. When you like something, you enjoy it more when you use the right word to describe it. Let's face it. Everything you describe isn't actually *wonderful* or *terrific!* To be really *wonderful,* it should fill you with honest wonder. That candy you're eating can't be *terrific*—the best it can do is to taste good.

So be on your guard. If you go overboard with adjectives too frequently, you'll probably end up like Pat. She's the girl who'll "simply die" if she can't have a date with Tom. She's "wild" about this; and "hysterical" about that. Pat, you'd better take it easy! People aren't listening to you any more. You would be wise to memorize this verse, then put it into immediate use: "Let your speech be alway with grace, seasoned with salt, that ye may know how ye ought to answer every man" (Col. 4:6). Supercharged words lose their power when they're overworked.

One sure mark of a poised, self-confident person is his ability to express himself with precise, well-chosen words. Colorful, fresh words, of course—and full of meaning—but not full of exaggeration. "Be not rash with thy mouth (let your words be few) . . . a fool's voice is known by multitude of words" (Eccl. 5:2, 3).

And then there's *slang.* What about it? Are there rules against it?

Not exactly. But for the most part we could do without it. Slang is usually a poor substitute for an authentic word. An overdose of slang sounds cheap and unrefined. Yet there are times when it can be particularly expressive. Some words such as "umph" or "jitters," or some phrase like "on the ball," are almost irreplaceable. But if you find you are relying on such expressions constantly, better try expanding your vocabularly with some strong, clear-cut English. Then, too, some slang falls into the near-swearing category— "heck, gosh, darn, gee-so," and such. These words have no place in the vocabulary of a Christian. Why not join the psalmist in his desire: "Let the words of my mouth, and the meditation of my heart, be acceptable in thy sight, O Lord, my strength, and my redeemer" (Ps. 19:14).

How many words do you know? Chances are you know many more than you are using. Why not try putting all the words you know to work, and then start expanding your vocabulary? Don't moan. Developing a good vocabulary doesn't mean laboriously reading "so many pages" of the dictionary each day. But it does mean looking up any unfamiliar words that you may read or hear. Many students reserve one page in a notebook so that they can jot down new or unusually effective words. After using them a few times, these words *belong* to them.

One word of warning. Don't start using stilted, unsuitably large words. After all, the object of speaking is to have people *understand* you. The best idea is to speak naturally, using good basic English. But know enough words so that you can occasionally enrich your conversation with some fresh and meaningful words.

When you know *how* to say it, the chances are, people will *want* to hear it.

Two-Way Talk

How do we start the conversational ball rolling?

It usually comes naturally. But if it doesn't, you can always ask a question. Just remember to ask something that has to do with the other fellow's interests.

If you play center on the basketball team and you meet Joe, lead man of the school's debating society, a question like: "Hi, Joe, how did the debate go, Friday?" is a much better beginning for a conversation than—"Say, did you see the basketball game last Saturday night?"

Then *listen* to what Joe has to say. And *look* at him while you listen. Your attentive silence will show that you are interested. Listening will help to make you a better conversationalist. Not only will you be *learning* from what you hear—but you'll win the admiration of others. In short, *to be interesting is to be interested.*

If Joe is smart, he'll bring you in on the conversation just as soon as he can. He'll know that a good talking partner never "over-talks" the other fellow. A good technique to use in drawing the other person into the conversation is to ask some well-put questions that have to do with *his* ideas and interests. For the most part, forget about what you'd like to say—and concentrate on what *he'd* like to say. It really works.

Do you ever find yourself in the spot where you don't know what to say? Everyone else around you is talking—but you are lost in silence.

That's no fun. Perhaps this situation could be remedied if you'd work on restoring your information department! Did you come across a phrase you liked? Then jot it down. When you hear a clever idea, file it away in a corner of your mind. It may come in handy later. Good jokes are always fun to repeat—but by all means, get the punch line straight. When the right time comes, and if you have these conversational helps stored away in your mind, you'll be glad that you have something worth-while or appropriate to say. Saying the right thing at the right time is fun.

Is conversation a lost "art"? It doesn't need to be. You can be a "top flight" conversationalist if you'll follow these few simple rules:

—Show a genuine interest in others. People will love you for it.
—Have something interesting to say—and then say it well.
—Talk about the Lord. There is no better subject.
—Never tell shady stories and avoid touchy subjects.
—Talk with a smile — be cheerful and optimistic. No "wet blankets" please!
—Be able to discuss differences of opinion without getting disturbed. Heated discussions are *out!*

59

—Wait your turn. Never interrupt while someone is talking. Two people talking at once is most confusing—and useless. Besides that, it's rude.

—Never monopolize a conversation. Remember, more than one person is involved. So give the others a chance, too.

—When you join a group, listen to the others a minute or two before you become a part of the conversation. Don't barge in with a new subject. See how skillfully you can blend into the group.

So — make your voice sound pleasant — let your words be well-chosen—encourage the other person to talk—and make the Lord the silent listener to every conversation. These are important secrets to your success!

6

GETTING ALONG WITH YOUR FAMILY

SEVERAL MONTHS BEFORE I started writing *Young Only Once* I met with various groups of young people. I asked them what they would like to have included in the book. "Give us some pointers on how to get along with our families," they said.

Getting along with parents requires real skill — a necessary skill. It's important because your success in life depends to a great extent upon how well you make out with your mother and father. Believe it or not, studies show that young people who have the best relationships with their parents also make the best citizens, the best husbands and wives, and the best business and professional men and women. Why is this? Because getting along with parents is one form of getting along with people in general. And skill in human relationships is important. No matter what you do, you can't get away from people—all kinds.

So, you see, if you learn how to get along with your family, you'll have little trouble getting along with anyone else.

"But," you say, "you don't know my folks. No one can please them. And besides, they aren't saved. What are you going to do in a case like that?"

I know that all parents aren't easy to live with. Some of them have never known the touch of the Savior in their lives. But such facts don't excuse you from settling down and doing *your* part to try to click with them. In fact, it's a challenge. If you are a Christian, God will give you grace and wisdom (provided that you ask for it). And if your parents are not believers, you may have the special privilege of leading them to the Lord. Thousands of other sons and daughters have done that very thing.

Chances are, your parents are fine, sensible people who love you more than you'll ever realize. But whether they are or not, the following suggestions will work—really work. They are not pulled out of a magician's hat. Rather, they are taken from the experiences of other young people just like you. Try them and you'll prove to yourself that you *can* get along with your folks after all, and in so doing, you'll become a much finer person yourself. Remember, parents are here to stay. They'll stick with you when the rest of your "friends" pull out on you. So their friendship is infinitely more valuable.

Remember God's first commandment with promise: "Honor thy father and thy mother: that thy days may be long upon the land which the Lord thy God giveth thee" (Exod. 20:12).

Talking It Over

Top level executives talk things over. The higher their position, the more time they spend in discussion. Why? Because it's the best way to solve problems and to make good decisions.

But it not only gets results in big corporations. It works just as well at home. Try it and see.

Words make good conditioners; they get people ready. They can relieve tensions and apprehensions. It helps to talk things out. That's why they have "gripe" sessions in the Army. It gives everyone a chance to unload and get things out in the open.

But be sure that your discussions are kept calm and friendly. Little is accomplished when you shout at each other or make hasty remarks. Getting excited when you are trying to talk things over is almost a sure way of losing your point. So by all means, keep sweet if you want to get anywhere.

As a Christian you must guard against bottled up differences that might clog the channels of your spiritual life. So learn to sit down with your parents and quietly talk things over. It will be time well spent— and one of the best ways to get along with your mother and dad.

Last Minute Plans

Don was sliding into his jacket and reaching for the front door as he called over his shoulder, "Hey, Dad! Bill and I planned to go to the game tonight. Mind if I use the car?"

You know what's wrong with this approach, don't you? That's right. You *sprang* it on him.

Your folks may not mind your taking the car, but they don't like these sudden surprises. How much better it is to share your doings with Mom and Dad! They love you and have a vital interest in you. That's why they like to feel that they have a part in your program. They find enjoyment in knowing about *your* fun.

Time is a terrific agent. So put it to work. It mellows and makes many things more acceptable. In fact, when your parents have had time to mull over an idea, they may even come to think that it was their own. People are like that.

Sensing Moods

There are times when Mother and Dad are worried, tired and emotionally upset. Nothing unusual. It happens in the best of families. Folks are just human, that's all.

Take Mom for example. She has to be all things to every member of the family.

"Mom, where is my shirt?" "Mother, what time are we going to eat?" "Mom, did anyone call?" And so it goes, day in and day out. Life is an endless merry-go-round of meals, dishes, clothes and a hundred other things. Because Mom is a person and not a machine, there may be times when she does not feel so well.

63

That's where you come in. "Mom," you say, "let Sis and I do the dishes tonight." See if her eyes don't light up with appreciation. There are so many ways you can help. Think of a few yourself.

There are probably times when the family finances are low and both your parents feel the pinch. This, obviously, is not the time to ask for some extra money.

Alert yourself to your parents' moods. It makes for better family relationships—it's one of the nicest things you can do.

Dad

Every Dad likes to feel that he is the head of the house (even if he isn't). Both God and society pretty much hold him responsible for the way things go in

the family. He pays the bills. There are the groceries, clothing, rent—and a thousand other expenses. And he's the general "fix-it" man. But how much thanks does he get for it? Most of the time Dad is just taken for granted. However, this doesn't mean that he wouldn't appreciate a little praise now and then.

So don't forget Dad! He really is a V.I.P.

When Junior and Mary were small, chances are Dad romped and played with them. They paid him plenty of attention then—(and remember Dad likes attention). But after they began to grow up, poor Dad — many times he was left out. Perhaps he was busy with his work, and besides, Mom may have been easier to talk to.

After awhile he began to feel like a spare tire—something hanging around just in case things went wrong.

Dad probably won't admit it, but deep down inside he resents it. He feels slighted. And to be honest, maybe he is. So by all means, don't forget Dad. He has some wonderful ideas when you take time to ask about them.

Remember, it pays to pamper Papa! Try it!

Family Fun

The Nelson family down the street has lots of fun! Family get-togethers, picnics, home movies, and swimming parties are some of the good times they will remember for all their lives.

Everybody admires a family that sticks together. And the family that *plays* together does *stay* together.

"Do you mean that I'm not supposed to spend time with my own friends?"

No, of course not! But *do* get together with the family part of the time. Let your parents have fun, too. That's the way to keep them young.

Time marches on. And parents can get pretty lonely when their "baby" grows up.

Of course no one wants to stay a baby! But spending some time with Mom and Dad is *not* a sign of immaturity: Rather, it indicates you are really "growing up." When you learn to consider your folks, you'll find that you not only will make them happy, but that you'll enjoy knowing them better yourself.

It Costs So Little

It was almost seven-thirty when Dick started for the front door. Dad asked: "Where are you going, son?"

"Oh, just down to the ball game."

"When will you be getting home?"

"I won't be late, Dad. After the game we'll probably stop for a hamburger. But I'll be home before eleven."

At eleven o'clock, Dad was beginning to wonder. Then the phone rang.

Dick's voice spoke on the other end of the line. "Dad, I'm sorry I'm late, but Pete's car went on the fritz and we haven't been able to get the crazy thing going. Pete thinks it's the automatic choke. He's disconnecting it now so I should be home in about thirty minutes."

See what a phone call can mean? It took the pressure off Dad. His son was thoughtful. Parents have sat in agony for hours, thinking the worst, because they haven't heard from their son or daughter. Cost? Only a *dime,* but it's worth many a dollar!

Pay as You Grow

"Oh, it was wonderful!" said Mrs. Lane to her neighbor. "Dan and Betty took us out last night. Harry and I were so proud of them."

What a thrill it is for Mom and Dad when young people grow up enough to take them out—perhaps for a bite to eat, and then pick up the check. And of course, there are also other ways to pay as you grow. Parents are really impressed with the fact that their sons and daughters are no longer children when they begin earning enough to buy their own socks or stockings or a sweater.

Want to give yourself a boost? Then offer your parents a few dollars to help pay expenses. Children need to be cared for; but adults pay their own way.

So when you take some responsibility for board and room, it is another way of saying, "I am growing up."

How about the car? Do you put gas in it after you borrow it?

When you pay your share with your own money, you have a greater appreciation for what you have, and your parents have a greater appreciation for you.

Manners at Home

Everyone looks up to the person who knows what to do and how to do it. And how proud your parents are when they see you acting well-mannered! It makes them feel that every hour they dedicated to you was worthwhile.

But "know how" doesn't just happen! It is developed at home. No parent likes to feel that he has failed to teach his son or daughter good manners. And if you don't demonstrate politeness and culture at home, your folks may not know that you *can* act right.

Do you want to make Mom and Dad happy? Then show them the courtesy and respect that is due them. Remember, they *are* your parents!

Battle Lines

How well do you get along at home? Do you have a happy, relaxed situation, or is there constant conflict? Continual disagreements can wear a person down. But what to do about it!

Have you thought much about these "battle lines" with your family? They can be formed *any* time. Most anything can become an issue when you're looking for a skirmish.

A "shooting-match" of arguments back and forth does no good for anyone. Someone's bound to get injured. Sometimes the casualties are heavy. If you're smart, you'll use strategy to dodge these "battle lines."

Especially avoid arguments with your parents. When a clash looms up, side step it with a pleasant answer. The Bible says, "A soft answer turneth away wrath."

Yes, we know that some parents can be pretty bull-headed and even unreasonable. But that doesn't take the responsibility away from you. Remember, Jesus said, "Blessed are the peacemakers: for they shall be called the children of God" (Matt. 5:9).

But how does one go about keeping peace? Try this: Use your ears more and your tongue less. When your parents raise a point that you disagree with, try this technique: Instead of expressing your point of view, ask them to explain theirs further. See if you can bring out the best in your parents. It may work miracles.

Try using these magic words: "I'm sorry." And then mean it!

See how good a diplomat you are. After all, home is a pretty important place. And since you live there, you have a responsibility to do all you can to make it happy.

Meeting Your Friends

The Wilsons have a general understanding in their home. Don and Jane always make it a point to let Mom and Dad get acquainted with their friends.

A board of review? No, hardly that. Mr. and Mrs. Wilson are wonderful parents who realize the importance of companionship. In reality, they are doing their son and daughter a lifetime favor. Parents can see things their children can't—strong and weak points both.

How about you? Do you bring your friends in to meet the folks—or do you always dash to the car at the sound of a honking horn? It's important for your parents to have a chance to get acquainted with your friends. This association fosters confidence—both in you and in your friends.

What You Have

Everyone likes nice things. But having things nice is more than just getting them. It's keeping them.

Do you feel that Mom and Dad are picking on you? "Hang up your clothes!"—"Straighten up your room!" —"Put your things away!"

It may sound that way, but really, they are not trying to be mean. They realize that this is the line between men and boys, little girls and women! Mature people know how to take care of their things.

Young children, of course, are not too responsible for their belongings. But adults are. Your parents will have much more respect for you if you can be trusted with the upkeep of your clothes, room and car. This is a good way to prove your maturity.

Coat of Arms

I was a tall, lanky freshman in college when I first learned about our family's "Coat of Arms."

After English class, I dashed into the dormitory and grabbed the letter in the mail box. It was from Mom! I quickly opened it, "fleeced" it to make sure that a check or a dollar bill wasn't slipped in somewhere, and then sat down to have a little "visit" with Mom.

She told me all about the plans for the family reunion on Thanksgiving Day. *Relatives,* I thought to myself. *Are they going to ruin my Thanksgiving again?* When I was younger, I had always liked family reunions, but recently they had become pretty boring.

You see, I had planned to be with some of my old pals Thanksgiving, then with a cute little date that evening. But the reunion would upset everything. So I sat right down and wrote Mom a letter asking if she wouldn't count me out this Thanksgiving.

But it didn't work! Mom wrote right back and explained that these family occasions were our "Coat of Arms."

"Coat of Arms?—An insignia denoting a person, or a family."

Hmmm, I mused. *The distinguished Narramore family!*

Well, Mom won and I did spend Thanksgiving with

69

my relatives—all forty-five of them! Of course, I saw my girl friend, too, but surprisingly enough, I had a real good time with the "clan."

Today as I look back, I realize that those family days were important. Parents, you know, like to feel that they have established family customs that are worth observing. These family get-togethers, conventions and customs are extremely important to mothers and dads. So don't be a "kill-joy" but try to get into the spirit of them. You'll probably find that it's really lots of fun—and something that will bring you and your folks closer together.

Your Parents' Advice

Once I was talking to a boy about his relationships with his parents. "Dr. Narramore," he said, "I never ask my folks anything. I don't think they know the answers."

Well, perhaps in his case he was right, but on the other hand, part of his problem was that he never asked them. Parents (as well as others), are flattered when you ask them for advice. Why? Because it makes them feel that you have confidence in them—that you really believe in them. And when you ask advice of your parents, you impress them with how smart you are — smart and grown-up enough to go to the right source to get the facts!

Although you may not always accept your parents' advice about certain things, it doesn't mean that they can't make excellent contributions in other areas. For example, an unsaved father might not be able to give good spiritual advice, but he may be able to give you excellent suggestions regarding the business world.

So if you haven't used this technique to help get along better with your parents, why not give it a try?

Words and Deeds

Perhaps you haven't given it much thought, but Mother and Dad like compliments, too. I'll let you in on a secret: By the time your parents have become old enough to have teenage sons and daughters, their morales may need a little lift. Most likely Dad's hairline is farther back than he wishes it were, and Mom —well, she may not be quite the striking beauty that she was the day she was elected campus queen. And both are probably fighting the "battle of the bulge"— and a losing battle at that.

So all the more, they need your words of compliment. By the way, this is an excellent way to get in their good graces.

But compliments work with everyone—not just your parents.

Whether your words are spoken or written, they mean just as much. Once when I was speaking to a group of college and high school young people at a summer Bible conference, a smart-looking girl told me, "Dr. Narramore, I have a hard time getting along with my parents. I don't know what's wrong but something is."

"Have you written them since you've been at camp?" I asked.

"No, I haven't."

"That's a good way to get on better terms with your parents. Write them a note and tell them how much you miss them. It will mean a lot to them."

She had never thought of this. Parents need to be loved, and what's more they need to be *told* they are loved. And of course, you are the one they want to hear it from. So don't forget to write when you are away from home. Then they will know you have not forgotten them.

Birthday time? How about a gift? Anniversary? A greeting card is always in order. It's the little things like this as well as everyday courtesies and thoughtfulness that help you to establish rapport with your folks.

And it will make *you* a much finer person, too.

And Thy House

The strongest cord of love between parents and children is a spiritual one. It's the basis of real fellowship.

If your parents are saved, you should praise God! If they are not, God has given you a mission field right at home. Parents can't resist the beautiful, Christ-centered life of a loving son or daughter. And regardless of the hopelessness of your home condition, God can do the seemingly impossible.

Unanswered prayer? Then search your life for elements that may hinder. As you yield yourself to Him, He will refine your life, and speak to your mother and dad through you. Surely, "He is not willing that any should perish" (2 Pet. 3:9). "Believe on the Lord Jesus Christ, and thou shalt be saved, *and thy house*" (Acts 16:31).

Your Brothers and Sisters

"Wait a minute," said Lucille to several of her campus friends. "Would you mind waiting just a moment while I make a phone call home?"

Lucille's friends got quite a different impression of her when they heard the conversation with her younger brother:

"Hello. Is that you, stupid? I want you to tell Mom something for me. . . . No! No, of course not, stupid. Where'd you ever get such a crazy idea? The next time you take a bath, you better wash your *brains,* too. They sure need it. What? . . . No! Didn't you hear me? I said, no! Boy, oh, boy, you must be the *original moron.* Listen! And get it straight! This is the last time . . ."

Most fellows and girls who don't have brothers and sisters wish that they had them. And many who *do* have them wish that they—well, they get along with them just about as well as Lucille gets along with hers.

Brothers and sisters are really important people. If God has blessed you with them, you're fortunate. If you learn how to live with them, they will not only bring you much happiness now, but later on as well.

Of course, in any home you can expect some inequalities. Since no one in your family is perfect, you can't expect a perfect situation. And if your brothers and sisters do not know the Lord, you have a special responsibility to live an exemplary life around them so that they will want to know your Savior, too.

Here are some questions that will help you take a candid look at your approach to those who also call your parents "Mom" and "Dad."

1. *Do you "tell" or "ask"?* People don't like to be told. They prefer being asked. Whether it's a command or not, it is always less offensive to "ask" brothers and sisters to do certain things.

2. *Do you show them special kindnesses?* One of the best ways to show a person that you do care for him is to give him something which represents a sacrifice on your part. Maybe it's a birthday gift or some other remembrance. But whether it's big or little it effectively says, "I think you're swell!"

3. *Do you criticize or compliment?* In any family there's always a little criticism. But in your family do you make it a point to compliment your brothers and sisters? Compliments have a way of relieving a competitive atmosphere. They pave the way for good feelings.

4. *Do you argue?* If you haven't discovered better ways of talking with your brothers and sisters than arguing, try this: Instead of arguing, cast yourself into a different role. (Here's your chance to be a psychologist!) Knowing that heated arguments only lead to more unfriendliness, ask your brother (or sister) to tell you more about how he feels. Give him plenty of line. Keep him talking about how he looks at it. And finally, he'll start seeing your side of the question even without your arguing it. This approach does two things—it eliminates many un-

pleasant arguments, and it makes your brother, or sister, feel better toward you after it's all over.

5. *Are you courteous?* Good manners, you know, start at home. It's important for you to let your family see how courteous you are. Home is the place to make "Please" and "Thank you" a part of everyday living.

6. *Do you pray for them?* Christians, you know, have an advocate with their Heavenly Father. This is your greatest source of strength. And you have a definite responsibility to pray for your family. So don't fail to pray regularly for your brothers and sisters. It will mean a lot in maintaining good relationships. Try it, and see how God blesses you— and them!

Home Sweet Home

These tips on getting along with your family are simple. And yet they work! So if you want to improve situations around your home, put the above suggestions into operation for a few months, then notice the difference.

Is your home important? It surely is. Thomas Jefferson expressed the feelings of millions when he said, "The happiest moments of my life have been the few which I have passed at home in the bosom of my family." These are not idle words. They were spoken by a man who had achieved world fame, a man who had received the highest honors the world could bestow. The happiest moments of his life were those spent with his family!

Your home can mean just as much to you if it is crowned with the blessings of God. And your responsibility is to do *your part.*

The family is ordained of God!

7

WISE, WISER, WISEST

"IF I HAD IT ALL to do over again I would get more education." You've heard people say this, haven't you? Frustrated adults? Yes. Because their education doesn't match the ability God has given them.

Just what is this "must" called education? Does a person have to go to college to be educated?

Not necessarily.

Education is more a matter of diligence with the talent you do have. But formal education may help to develop your innate abilities. It usually does. Christians have a responsibility to God to be the best informed, the best educated people possible.

It was Joseph Addison who said, "What sculpture is to a block of marble, education is to a human soul."

So don't think lightly of your high school and college days. These are the years that will *set the stage*— the years that will become the *foundation* for the rest of your life's work. It's like the foundation of a building. The kind and size of the building you can erect depends upon the foundation you lay. That's why it is especially important that you accomplish everything you possibly can. You're *Young Only Once!*

What About College?

"Why go to college?" Dan asks. "I doubt if it will do anything for me that hard work won't do. In fact, I figure that I'd be better off with a four year head start on my job."

The truth is, Dan *would* have a head start if he

didn't go to college. But the advantage lasts only a few years. Something like a Model T starting out a little ahead of the latest model Ford.

What does college *really* do?

First, it sets you apart as a person of *known ability*. An employer knows when he hires a college grad that his weak point is not his brains.

Then too, you as a college student have received *professional training*. This means that you have vastly increased your *usability* for various kinds of work. Most college grads can readily fit into various types of positions.

And what about *income?* Will you make more money as a college grad? Yes, you'll definitely profit financially. A person's lifetime income expectancy is far greater when he has a college degree. A study some years ago showed that the average high school graduate earned approximately $165,000 in a lifetime. But the average college graduate earned $268,000. Difference: $103,000. This makes college look like a worthwhile financial investment, doesn't it?

Finally, college helps you develop *social skills* and *friendships* that are truly stimulating and enriching. A college education can increase your *enjoyment of life* immeasurably.

It also furnishes you with *contacts* that you'll treasure for a lifetime. And these are some of the things that can't be added up in dollars.

Who Qualifies?

If you are not already in college, you may be asking, "But how does one know if he qualifies? College isn't meant for everyone, is it?"

All we need to do is to look at the college failure rate—and we have half of your answer. No, college is not for everyone. Definitely not.

But how about the many high school students who *could* have been successful in college, but who *didn't* attend? Statistics show that only about one-half of the high school students who qualify for college ever get there. So the question as to whether or not a person should attend college has been answered unsatisfactorily. And it's an important decision to make. Since college admission usually depends upon three factors, you might check yourself on them:

1. What is your *intelligence?* Your college aptitude? If you are in the top twenty-five percent of your class, you should seriously consider college.

2. What kind of *grades* do you make? The best single predictor of college success is your high school average.

3. What are your *strong subjects?* It helps to have your best grades in the "solids." These are English, science, math and social studies.

If you match up to these general standards, take a careful look at college. You may make a great discovery.

College With a Purpose

"That prof inspires me," Betty remarked. "I think I'll switch to History for my major."

So Betty did just that.

In her senior year Betty visited the placement office.

"Any jobs for a history major today?" she asked.

"What did you have in mind? Something in the secretarial line?"

"Heavens, no! I'm a college graduate; as of June, that is!" countered Betty sharply. "I want something in keeping with my education and study."

But it wasn't that simple. And Betty suddenly discovered that not all education leads to a job.

If Betty had taken some education courses along with the history, she could have become an educator. But unfortunately, many young people drift through college going nowhere except to classes. And at the end of four years they are not prepared for anything— jobwise.

What will your employability be? Better think now

while you're in preparation. Attending college should be purposeful—a getting ready for something definite.

Education You Can't Do Without

All keys are not made of metal. Some doors in life require the keys of a sound, basic education. And there is *some* education you can hardly do without.

Take, for example, in marriage! When you take that big step, what kind of a mate will you be? Dull and uninteresting? Or alert and well informed? What do you know about biological factors, planning for children, economic and legal obligations and the basic elements of a sound marriage? Thousands of couples needlessly spend painful hours in divorce courts and psychiatrists' offices. Why? Because they lacked important family life education.

And what about *homemaking?* Steak every night for dinner might be fun—but catastrophic to the budget. Budgeting, sewing, planning meals and keeping up the home are items vital to every woman's education. A housewife needs a world of information.

Not infrequently is she called upon to support the family while her husband recovers from an illness or an accident. No one anticipates these things — but sometimes they happen. It's a good idea for a wife to have at least one marketable skill to keep in reserve for just such emergencies.

Another kind of education you can hardly do without is *child growth and development.* Your success later on as a mother, father, or teacher depends upon your knowledge of scientific facts about children. Whether a child develops into a misfit or a well-adjusted person depends largely upon your education and skill to guide him. This type of education is too important to miss. Children—who will become adults —are at stake.

And then there are other keys to life that may seem more obvious.

Typing and speech, for example. Who leads your

youth group? Not the chap who can never say what he means.

Who picks up those extra dollars typing term papers, manuscripts, or correspondence? Only the typist. Skill in typing is useful to nearly everyone. These seemingly simple skills can make you a much more effective and happy person.

But the most important key in life is a rich knowledge of *God's Word*.

Think of Tim. He plans to be a farmer—taking over part of his Dad's large farm. Does he need a college degree? He may or may not. But one thing *is* certain. Like *all* Christian fellows and girls, he needs to be educated in God's Word. So Tim decided to go to Bible college for at least one year. There he can become grounded in the Word so that he will be more useful as a Sunday school teacher, a men's leader, a soul winner and a well-informed Christian.

Every Christian needs Bible training. And a Bible school or a Christian college is an excellent place to get it.

Finances and Education

"Where will I get enough money for college?"

Is this the big question with you? Some people feel that they should have all the money needed for the entire four years of college before they start in.

But this isn't true.

God has promised to supply our needs, not for the next year, not for the next two years or three, but for today. If you have enough money for the first semester's expenses so that you can get by without working too much outside of school, you are well on your way. Step out in faith and trust in God.

By means of a part-time job or financial assistance from parents or friends you can probably get enough money to complete the rest of the year. Go step by step. Take a semester at a time. If you can successfully make it through the first semester, even if you must stop temporarily, you will find that one semester's work is to your credit. It can be transferred. So go as far as you can on the right road, and God will help you go a little further.

Don't hesitate to check into the possibility of a scholarship. You might find a real financial resource. Each year over half of the scholarships in the nation are unclaimed! Some are fairly large sums. Furthermore, not all scholarships are for the fair-haired, genius type of individual. Most are given to students who have a will to work and a definite purpose in mind. So check with your favorite school about this. Ask your local P.T.A. Your chances may be better than you think.

Marriage and Education

Joe and Eileen were sophomores at the State University. Deeply in love, and a bit starry-eyed, they planned to be married in the summer. Their parents thought they should wait, but Joe and Eileen won out. The wedding took place in beautiful fashion. Two blissful weeks of honeymoon, and then—back to school.

To support his bride, Joe took an evening job. After all, he wanted to keep Eileen looking like the queen that she was. Then before long they discovered that a baby was on the way. With Joe away evenings, and doctor bills mounting, some of the bliss began to vanish. Soon there were disagreements — and honest-to-goodness arguments. It was evident that their marriage was in conflict with Joe's education. Although Eileen's Dad offered to lend them some money, Joe wouldn't hear of it. He felt that if he was old enough to get married, he was old enough to pay his own way.

Eileen thought that if she had to quit for the sake of the baby, then why couldn't Joe do the same? "Besides," she argued, "we are going to need more money. The apartment won't be big enough, and we could use some new clothes." And maybe she was right!

What to do?

Although more and more college students are married while in school, the drop-out rate among them is high. Marriage and undergraduate education do not mix too well.

It's hard to believe when you're in love, but actually your marriage can wait more easily than your education. Those who leave college because of marriage responsibilities find it extremely difficult to return and finish their work. Usually, they never make it back, even though they may have left with the best of intentions to continue college later.

The story wouldn't have such an unhappy ending if a couple merely left college, then settled down to daily work and married life. But as a psychologist who counsels with many young married couples, I often see a more unfortunate outcome. The ambitious fellow or girl who starts to college, then drops out for marriage, is *not content to settle down without an education*. The result? Frustration that finds no solution; and frustration that keeps one from fully enjoying his daily work and his family.

So, you see, the safest and most reasonable arrangement is to get your education first. The additional years you spend in college add greatly to your maturity. You will then have much more to offer your partner.

So plan carefully and prayerfully. God rewards those who are patient and wait for His leading. "I will instruct thee and teach thee in the way which thou shalt go: I will guide thee with mine eye" (Ps. 32:8).

Be Sure It's Christian

There was a time when an institution that advertised itself as a Christian college was really what it claimed to be. But unfortunately, that's not always true today.

A genuinely Christian institution is one in which the president and every member of the faculty are born-again believers, and where the Bible is upheld as the

81

inspired Word of God. In such a college, there is constant, special emphasis on soul winning.

Some church-sponsored colleges that are no longer thoroughly evangelical know the "language" well enough to fool many innocent "suckers." They cleverly place certain phrases in their advertising so that the casual reader won't suspect the fact that they are really not evangelical institutions. So we must be on our guard and not become involved in any counterfeit "Christian" college.

Personal Interest

There is nothing quite so wonderful and stimulating as knowing that those around you are interested in you, desiring that you do well.

This is characteristic of a Christian school. Non-Christian institutions try to develop this quality, too, but teachers who do not know Christ cannot possibly have the same devotion to their students as those who know Christ. Only those who are indwelt by the Holy Spirit can appreciate the tremendous potential of another child of God.

Most administrators and teachers in Christian colleges could teach at a non-Christian institution and receive a much higher salary. But their devotion to Christian young people means more to them than personal gain. You see, they are more interested in helping you than they are in making more money. Why? Because it is a service unto the Lord.

You, as a Christian student, can attend a non-Christian college almost unnoticed; whereas, in a Christian institution you would be considered worthwhile.

Courses of Study

The types of courses offered at Christian schools are usually about the same as those offered anywhere.

Most universities and colleges emphasize certain general courses such as English, science, foundations of education, psychology and sociology. These are generally required. During the freshman and sophomore years, one is usually not permitted to take many courses of his own choice. This same policy is followed in both Christian and secular colleges.

If the course you expect to pursue is sufficiently specialized to require undergraduate courses at specific schools, you can still attend the first two years at a Christian college. Then transfer later. This will give you at least two wonderful years in a Christian environment.

Quality of Scholarship

The teachings of a Christian college are usually more factual and accurate than those of a non-Christian institution. Christian teachers have access to secular knowledge, and in addition, they have spiritual understanding, that non-Christians do not have. For example, history cannot be accurately interpreted apart from God's dealings with man. Psychology goes far afield unless it is Christ-centered. Science is likely to be guesswork if professors ignore God's work. And so it goes.

Standards in Christian institutions are usually equal and sometimes superior to non-Christian schools. But even more important is the Christian understanding and spiritual application that is integrated with the facts learned.

Friendships

Everyone wants and needs friends.

The friendships one develops at Christian colleges and Bible schools meet this need. A few years from now you will appreciate the fact that we live, to a great extent, by our Christian contacts. The evangelical, Christian work of America, has a strong element of unity.

God uses Christians to help other Christians, and it is seldom that a man has an extensive work for the Lord unless he has a wide acquaintance with those of like precious faith. These friendships are easily made and cultivated in Christian schools.

Dating

Dating a non-Christian is dangerous business.

That is why you, as a college student, should have the opportunity to meet many other Christians your age with whom you can have good times and fellowship, and from whom you can choose your life's partner. To be frank, the "picking" is often slim in non-Christian colleges where there may be only a handful of Christians.

It is not enough for a Christian to marry another Christian. One should have sufficient choice to marry the Christian.

Only recently I counseled with Nancy and Bill, a

84

young couple who were having a difficult time in their marriage. They had followed the scriptural teachings of not being unequally yoked together with an unbeliever. But the tragedy was that although they were both believers, they were *not* married to the right believer.

Frequently this situation can be easily traced to the fact that Christian young people who do not attend a Christian college have such a small circle of Christian friends that they seldom have an opportunity to find a life partner who is really suited to them.

Christian Conduct

It's more than book knowledge—it's what you learn by living!

That's where a Christian college has no competition.

There you learn the joy of total dedication to Christ. It is there that you rise above worldly standards and reach a place in Christian experience where God can use you mightily. Do you want the joy of living out-and-out for Christ? Are you looking for the blessings that accompany true consecration? At a fine Bible institute or Christian college it is the natural way of life.

Of course, one need not attend a Christian school to learn surrender and dedication. But a fine, evangelical institution helps one develop into a consecrated Christian, a spiritual giant whom God can use!

Knowledge of the Scriptures

The Bible commands us to hide God's Word in our hearts. That means "study."

Outstanding Bible scholars teach required Bible courses. The nation's outstanding laymen and ministers speak at chapel programs.

The ideal time to learn the Word of God thoroughly is when you are a young person. In middle and later life you will be so occupied with family and business responsibilities that you may not follow through with intensive Bible study.

If one doesn't build thorough Bible knowledge into his life in his teens and early twenties, he may never do it. And to neglect such training is to disregard the most important preparation for life!

Learning God's Will

God has a unique plan for each life. He has one for you.

The successful Christian diligently seeks God's will for his life. For the most part, God uses natural means of showing us His will.

There is no place where a young person can learn about the opportunities of Christian service as well as he can in a Christian school.

There the needs of the various mission fields are carefully presented. Student groups are organized to learn more about the opportunities of Christian service.

Harold, an earnest Christian, attended an outstanding Bible school. During his time there he heard a challenging message from a man who was engaged in home and camp work for delinquent boys. After the chapel service he talked with the speaker. Harold prayed much about the work and later felt led to enter it. God blessed him in his decision, and today he is doing a great work for God.

Witnessing

Have you ever heard the claim that a person has more opportunities for witnessing on a non-Christian campus?

Let's look into it and see if it is really sound logic.

Nearly every evangelical Christian school has an organized program whereby all students learn to witness in many situations, and with various groups. They visit in hospitals, witness in jails, pass out tracts on streets, give testimonies at meetings, preach at various nearby services, make house-to-house contacts and take part in many other such activities. Actually, most students attending Christian colleges engage in witnessing much more than those Christians attending non-Christian institutions. And such activities in a Christian school are consistent and well-planned.

Many Christian colleges even encourage a summer program whereby students keep accurate records of their witnessing opportunities and then register them with school officials from week to week.

Away From Home

Going away to a Christian college usually means getting away from home. It means leaving Mom and Dad and your old friends.

Many times this is good for you.

Unfortunately, too many Christian young people never leave their parents until they get married. As wonderful as it is to have the influence of godly parents, it is also advantageous to be in a fine Christian college environment where one cannot turn to Mother or Dad for every decision. This helps you to stand on your own two feet, to become self-reliant and independent.

Many parents, desiring to do the best for their children, are not aware that they are dominating them, and to some extent robbing them of their own development. Leaving Mother and Dad is not a virtue in itself, unless one gets into a spiritual atmosphere such as that provided by a Christian college.

There are great numbers of young people whom God could use if they would be willing to leave Main Street in their own home town. Going away to school introduces you to new cultures and different climates. It opens the curtain to new vistas and permits you to see greater challenges in Christian service.

Maximum Development

We do not grow through resistance. We grow when we take part.

That is why the heart of Christian college activity centers in individual development.

A tree that is planted in poor soil doesn't have

nearly the chance as the one planted in good earth. Children do not develop because they resist food. Just as a swimmer needs to get into the water, so young Christians need spiritual activity.

1. In non-Christian colleges you cannot take part in many of the activities because they are not suitable for Christians. Dancing, drinking, smoking, off-color stories and a thousand other things are the regular diet for unregenerate collegians. In fact, in some colleges it is extremely difficult to hold student body offices unless you go along with all these activities.

2. You don't grow by refusing to participate. So, go to a Christian college where you can participate.

If more young people realized the danger of mixing with the godless gang, they would give more thought to attending a Christian college where every activity is Christ-centered.

Christ Himself took His disciples aside where they would be unmolested by worldly interference. Surely your college days are times of learning and preparation. Where could you better be than with the Lord's people in a Christian institution where you and other Christian young people grow strong for God and country?

8

YOUR LIFE'S WORK

EVERYONE WANTS to be successful in his vocation or profession. And of course, you do.

But do you have a *plan* for success? In what direction are you heading? Let's take a long look at some of the things that will help make you *successful!*

God gives all Christians a basis for living: "In Him we live, and move, and have our being" (Acts 17:28). This means that God is interested in *you*. He is actually the center—the hub of all that you do. Since God truly wants you to make the most of your life, then certainly He must have a *plan* for you. If God created you, surely He is far better able to order your life than you are. So trust Him for guidance and you will be much more successful than you ever could be if you relied upon yourself. "Trust in the Lord with all thine heart; and lean not unto thine own understanding. In all thy ways acknowledge him and he shall direct thy paths" (Prov. 3:5, 6).

"But," you say, "I'm not going to be a preacher or a missionary."

Perhaps not. But God isn't speaking only to ministers and missionaries. He is speaking to *you*. In fact, *God is more desirous for you to be successful than you are yourself*. In the Bible we find that God is so interested in people that He gives them personal commands.

Look at Peter—a mere fisherman. But before God was through with him, Peter was a "fisher of men." The Lord Jesus came to Peter personally and drew him away from his leaky boat and smelly fish. What an amazing transformation — from a common fisherman to a great apostle!

And God has not changed. He is just as interested in you as He was in Peter.

No man has to accept a second best for his life. There's a place for *every* man, and it's his own fault if he misses it.

Success? There's only one *real* way to atttain it. And that is to be in the will of God!

How Can I Tell What My True Abilities Are?

As I counsel with young men and women, I find that many people are square pegs in round holes. They are not happy in their life's work because they are not doing the thing for which they are best suited. Their work is not a joy. It is drudgery.

"But," you ask, "how can I know what I am really capable of doing? I don't want to be a misfit."

Of course you don't! And you don't need to be.

Today there are some excellent ways to determine where your abilities lie and what type of work would probably be most suitable for you. The choice of your life's work doesn't need to be guesswork.

Let's take a look at the men and women who have climbed the ladder of success. Here is their advice on how to discover your real talents.

1. *Take Aptitude Tests*

Aptitude tests are designed to indicate your native interests and abilities. They are used by industry, by many professions and by the Armed Forces. You can arrange to take aptitude tests and interest inventories at school. Those who are not enrolled in school can get reliable information about them by phoning the administrative office of a local high school or college.

2. *Consult Your School Advisor*

Guidance specialists in schools are usually walking encyclopedias of vocational knowledge. Get acquainted with them. Talk with your own counselor about your future plans (or lack of them). He will be happy to discuss your problem and to give you helpful literature.

3. *Take Inventory of Any Special Talents You May Have*

Take a careful look at your talents, even if they are small, and even if they are not yet developed. God gives you talents to *use. Talents are God's suggestions for your life's work.* It's amazing how you can use your talents if you are in His will.

If you are uncertain about the extent of your talent, talk with your teachers or with people already in professional work. They are likely to have a realistic point of view.

4. *See Where Your Interests Lie*

What kinds of work do you like? This is an indication of what you *should* do. Some people are "naturals." This means that they are doing work in which they have real ability and which they thoroughly enjoy.

5. *Take a Vocational Guidance Course*

Vocational guidance courses are set up for the specific purpose of informing you as to what jobs are available, and as to what their requirements are. They also help you assess your own ability.

If possible, enroll in such a course.

6. *See Vocational Films*

Interesting, reliable films have been made of nearly all major professions and vocations. These are free for your viewing. School counselors are anxious to show them to you.

Professional men and women in your community can also advise you as to where you can see films describing their type of work.

7. *Read Literature on Various Occupations*

Librarians in every community and school can show you excellent books that discuss various professions

91

and vocations. Excellent literature on vocations is also available in school guidance offices and at most bookstores. Take a look at it. You'll get some valuable information this way.

8. *Talk With Men in Various Professions*

Some of the best sources of vocational information are men and women you know. Strike up a conversation with them. See how gladly they will talk about their line of work. What's more, they'll undoubtedly invite you to visit them at work so you can get more firsthand understanding.

9. *Check Your School Grades*

How are your grades? They tell a fairly accurate story about your ability. As you consider your success or failure in certain courses, you can benefit from what teachers think about your ability and achievement.

10. *Explore the Field — Take Part-time Jobs*

Part-time jobs do more for you than merely provide you with some income. They give you actual, on-the-job experience. This is invaluable. So look around and try various jobs on for "size." You'll soon know which one is, or isn't for you.

11. *Consider Your Health*

Your future may be partially determined by your health. Face up to your attributes or handicaps, learn to accept them and get into the kind of work that is most suitable. Then you'll be happy.

12. *Pray for Guidance*

The greatest guidance of all is from God. If you are in His will, He will lead you into the paths He wants you to follow. He will open and close doors. If you are in close fellowship with Him, He will answer your prayers. The answers may be "yes" or "no." They may come through normal circumstances, through the Bible, or other sources. But they will be God's best for you!

Here's a thrilling fact: Among the millions of human beings in the world, no two are alike. Each is unique. The same is true of nature. Just as God has a design in every snowflake, every leaf, so He has a plan for you! If you take every advantage of the suggestions above, and earnestly commit your life to Christ, He will, in His time, reveal His perfect plan for you.

Conflict of Being Interested in Several Fields

"What should a person do when he is interested in more than one vocation?"

If this is your problem, you have lots of company. Many young people face this situation. In fact, studies of gifted individuals show that they are usually talented in more than one field. The studies also show that the more abilities you have, the longer it may take you to reach a decision about your life's work.

The average student changes his mind three or four times while he is attending college. Does this sound like you? Furthermore, many college graduates take positions in certain fields, then change vocations completely later on.

93

"Oh," but you ask, "doesn't God call a person to a certain type of work expecting him to stay in it?"

No, not always. God may lead you in various directions so that you will develop several of your abilities. Eventually you may cement them all together into one picture, using these varied experiences as a background for still another type of work. The late Dr. V. Raymond Edman was a good example. He served as a pastor, a teacher and a missionary. Then God called him to be the president of one of our great Christian colleges.

Just be sure that at each stage of your life you are where God wants you to be. Then He will lead you in His perfect will.

Conflict With Parents in Vocational Plans

A young man once asked, "What shall I do? My parents want me to be an engineer but I want to be a missionary."

He had a real problem. But it was not an uncommon one. Many young people encounter similar conflicts.

Why is this? Not because parents do not love their children. On the contrary, they are vitally interested in them. And that, many times, is what causes the "rub."

Some parents unknowingly try to live out their unfulfilled ambitions through their sons and daughters. Their children become a source of vicarious accomplishment—a secondhand realization of their own hopes and dreams.

"But this isn't fair," you say. "I've got my own life to live!"

You're right. But don't brush off your parents too quickly. Talk with them about it. A calm discussion of any problem is always helpful. Rest assured that if you trust God, He will work it out in His own time.

Sometimes it is difficult for a parent who has climbed up the occupational ladder to imagine his son or daughter taking a job of lower prestige than his own. Or perhaps your parents are tied to you. Apron strings can be attached on both ends, you know. Or maybe it's the location of the job that causes concern. It's only natural for parents to like to have their children where they can visit them. So you can understand *why* they may feel the way they do.

But whatever the conflict, find out if the reasons are God-centered or self-centered. Your first allegiance is to God. Make up your mind on that basis. He will take care of the rest.

Salaries

You may have heard about the gang of little boys who decided to have some fun. So one night they climbed through the transom of a hardware store—and then things began to happen! Through the store they ran, switching the price tags of all the merchandise. Bicycles were twenty-nine cents each. Television sets were two cents a pound. Nails became $79.95 a piece. Cork stoppers sold for $6.98. What a time the poor store owner had the next morning when his customers saw the confusion of prices!

But is this so different from life? We live in a society that has paid a "glamorous," degenerate movie star a million dollars for one film. With a raucous voice and jungle rhythm, she makes a fortune with degrading music.

On the other hand, a godly missionary may spend years preparing himself in medicine or theology. How much will he earn? Perhaps a measly few thousands a year! Yet his services can only be measured in terms of eternity.

It sounds like a switch in price tags, doesn't it? *Satan has switched the price tags* in this world, and they will not be straightened out until the Lord returns!

Seldom is there much relationship between the eternal value of a job and the price tag placed upon it. Great men of God are not highly paid in money.

"Does this mean that I should always take a job with a low salary?"

No, not necessarily. If you are in God's will, you'll want the job that is best for you.

This may help you: If you were offered three jobs, you might ask yourself, "If all three positions were in the same location, if they all paid the same salary and if they all offered equal prestige, which one would I take?" This simple test has helped many Christians know God's will for them.

Finding a Job and Keeping It

"How does one go about *finding* a job?"

If you are completing your training, the placement bureau at your school can undoubtedly help you locate the job you want. Private and public employment agencies also assist the right man to get the right job. And don't overlook the advertisements in the newspaper. All of these various means can help you immeasurably.

You will likely use a combination of these job-finding methods. Most people do. But this is only the beginning. When you've found the job you *want, getting* it will depend on how well you can sell yourself to the employer.

Letter of Application

Occasionally you may find it necessary to write a letter of application. And naturally, it is important. Your letter of application is really a picture of yourself and what you can do. So put your best "type" forward: Make it sharp and clear. Show your qualifications at their best by sending a neat, carefully typed, perfectly spelled letter.

Be factual. Be sure to include your name, age, address, and telephone number; as well as the obviously important educational background, special training and experience.

Be positive. Never start your letter with this negative approach: "I don't suppose I will qualify for the position, but I . . ."

Do say: "In June I will graduate from Ohio State University. For the past three years I have majored in electrical communication and related fields. Consequently, your company interests me. Would it be . . ."

Be brief. A large company receives thousands of applications each year; so a brief, to the point letter is attractive to the personnel office.

Brief, positive and factual! Then send your letter on its way. If it does a good job of telling who you are and what you can do, and if you seem to meet the qualifications required for the job, you will soon be called for an interview.

The Interview

This is it. The personnel man is to see you in a few minutes.

Perhaps you are a little tense or nervous. That's only natural. You probably realize that most jobs are either won or lost in these few minutes in the interviewer's office. And yet, a little intelligent preparation goes a long way toward putting you at ease. So by all means, know what you're doing!

As you sit in the waiting room breathe another prayer in your heart that God will open and close doors according to His divine plan. Your job should be just as sacred to you as the foreign field is to the missionary. You only want the job if God so wills it.

Before you leave your house, consider how you should look when you step into the personnel office. Plan what you might say. It will send you to your interview with more self-confidence and assurance; and a better chance of getting the job.

What about your appearance? Look at yourself. Are you clean? Neat? Clothes pressed? Shoes polished? Hair in place? This is more important than you think. An employer is afraid to trust exacting work to an untidy person.

Now take a look at your posture. No slouching, no leaning against a wall or desk for support if you want to appear mentally alert, healthy and energetic. Whether you are sitting or standing, straighten your backbone. It will help you look vitally alive and ambitious.

It's a wonderful asset to be prepared when you step into the personnel office. Let your interviewer give you your cues. If he is talking on the phone, wait quietly by the door until he speaks to you. If he offers to shake hands—do it. If he suggests you sit—then sit. And when he is ready the questions will begin. Remember, your ability to answer definitely and intelligently is of tremendous importance. Make your answers direct, accurate and courteous. Don't try to bluff; you won't fool anyone but yourself. Keep your troubles to yourself. The interviewer is not there for a counseling session.

Be alert to realize when the interview is over, and be prompt to leave. Your interviewer has your telephone number, and he will notify you if he decides you are the one for the job. So relax and pray for the best!

Much to Learn

Congratulations! The job is yours.

But this is just the beginning: There's much to learn. The first few days on any job seem to be an almost overwhelming blur of new names, strange procedures and innumerable directions. But the haziness of a new job will quickly clear if you relax and let yourself learn. Remember, no one expects you to know everything the first day—but it is important that you catch on quickly. So here are a few hints.

Listen! Don't be so overcome with your anxiety to succeed that you do not hear directions accurately.

Ask! When you don't understand exactly, ask for an explanation. Asking will show that you are sincerely interested in learning. Of course, be sure you choose a suitable time for your question.

Admit Mistakes! If you make an error don't wait for someone to call it to your attention. Explain your error to your superior and then correct it according to his suggestions. This will show that you understand your job, and that you are sincere about it. Your fellow workers will respect you for your honesty.

Attentive listening, careful watching, and well-timed asking will give you a good start on your new job. Chances are, if you are truly interested and do your best, the job will be yours as long as you want it.

Getting Ahead

"Is there any future in this job?" you may wonder.

Usually the future is *not* in the job: rather, it is in the man who *holds* the job.

So if you're anxious to get ahead, the challenge is there. Your first job is seldom an end in itself: it is a stepping stone to a higher position. It's up to you. A number of personnel men have made these "getting-ahead" suggestions:

1. Do what you are asked, and be willing to do more.
2. Write things down. Mental notes have a way of becoming fuzzy.
3. Don't brag about knowing the vice-president. Just work to improve your own abilities.
4. Avoid arguments. Don't take every remark as a personal insult. Personality clashes are a more common cause for dismissal than inability to do the job.
5. Be friendly, but take your time. Don't tell a fellow worker your life history the first week you are on the job.
6. Don't gossip. If you overhear something, don't repeat it.
7. Look your best. Dress suitably for your position. Neat, clean and *right*.
8. Be punctual. Get to work on time, and be back from lunch when you are due.

9. Don't underestimate the importance of your work. Do it well, and it adds to your company's fine reputation. Do it poorly, and it weakens your job and your firm as well.

10. Learn your company's procedures and policies. Such understanding makes you a valuable employee.

Getting ahead is largely up to you. Some people vaguely hope for success tomorrow.

But why wait? You can begin your success today!

Great Challenges of the Century

The best job for you is the one to which God calls you. And of course you can witness for Him wherever you are.

But there are some professions today that are especially significant because there are so few Christians in them, and because the opportunities to influence many people are great.

Here are several fields of service which seem to me to be especially significant. Perhaps God would have you enter one of them.

Social Service

It was Tuesday afternoon and Mr. and Mrs. Parker were at home anxiously awaiting the arrival of the county social worker.

Their adoption application had been in process for nearly three years, and now at last they had hopes of adopting a baby!

The social worker arrived, talked pleasantly with the Parkers, then assured them that their application would receive attention in due time. But little did the Parkers realize that the unsaved social worker would submit a "not recommended" report, since the Parkers were "religious fanatics" with peculiar religious plaques on their walls—"evidently maladjusted."

Unregenerate workers in the field of social service

100

are making important decisions and influencing multitudes of people—and without spiritual wisdom!

This great field of social welfare which should be of special concern to evangelical Christians has been sorely neglected by them. Unfortunately, the church, which was originally given the responsibility to care for the needy, has in the course of time allowed its obligation to drift over into the hands of civic organizations and non-Christian welfare groups.

Although requirements vary slightly in different states, most state welfare organizations require that caseworkers have a master's degree in social service beyond their regular bachelor's degree. In some instances, this master's degree is received after one year of training in school (beyond college graduation) followed by one year of practical experience. In other cases two years of training are required, part of that period being spent in a supervised field.

The field is wide open; the need is so great and heartbreaking that it should stir the heart of any believer who truly loves the Lord. It calls for hard work and constant application. It has its disappointments and difficulties—but it is one of the kinds of work to which our Lord called His people.

Education

If you want to influence America, you should go where the *people* are, and where they are *young*. This means the public schools. The teachings of the classroom soon become the beliefs of the average citizen. If the teachers and school administrators of our nations are godly men and women, their beliefs and attitudes will quickly become a part of the young lives whom they influence.

As an educator your clientele will be the youth of the nation. And in many cases, you will be associated with boys and girls during more hours each day than will their parents or any other person.

As an educator you will be the interpreter of in-

101

formation and knowledge. You will be in a position to constantly emphasize Christian truths. You will mold the students' habits, attitudes and ideals.

You will also be a witness to other faculty members. Many educators are finding Christ through their professional associates.

The field of education offers a variety of professional careers. Here is a partial list: Kindergarten teacher, elementary teacher, secondary teacher, college instructor, counselor, speech therapist, psychologist, school nurse, business manager, registrar and supervisor.

There is a national shortage of educators. During the next two decades there will be a great demand to meet the increased population.

A career in education continues for a lifetime. Positions of importance become increasingly available with years of service and experience. You will become more valuable at fifty than you were at thirty.

There is a great organization of Christian educators called "The National Educators' Fellowship." This active group has local chapters and campus chapters throughout the nation. They have an excellent monthly magazine called *Vision*.

Psychology

Not long ago the superintendent of a large school district said: "Dr. Narramore, we are in need of a psychologist for our district. Can you suggest one we might interview?" A few days later another superintendent inquired: "Where can we get a good psychologist? The board feels we should employ such a man next fall." Shortly afterward my telephone rang. It was another administrator with the same question: "We need a psychologist for our school. This time we want a Christian. Whom do you suggest?"

To most of these questions I have to say, "There are hardly *any* Christian psychologists available."

What a pity that such strategic positions cannot be filled by Christian men!

For many obvious reasons elementary schools, secondary schools and colleges are employing full time psychologists much as they do nurses, attendance officers and business managers. Although the field is open to both men and women, it is much easier for a man to be placed. School psychologists have many responsibilities such as case studies of individual students; working with parents, and counseling with students, teachers and administrators. They also provide in-service training for teachers. They develop programs of preventative mental health, and set up programs for the gifted, retarded and handicapped.

In fact, a well-trained psychologist is not only valuable in a given school district, but also in the community. He has many opportunities to speak to unsaved groups and to lead people to Christ. People come to him for help and willingly follow his suggestions. What an opportunity to serve our Lord Jesus Christ!

People sometimes ask, "What kind of person makes a good school psychologist?" Undoubtedly he should be: Someone who goes *toward,* not *away* from people. A person who is radiant, happy and well adjusted. Someone who is sufficiently intelligent to study, get advanced degrees, and work with other intelligent people. Someone whose appearance is sufficiently good to enable him to work intimately with others. A person who understands education. And most important, one who knows the Word and loves the Lord Jesus Christ!

As for requirements: Most states require an undergraduate major in education (preferably elementary because that is where most of the openings are), and a strong minor in psychology. One must also have a master's degree in educational psychology. Teaching experience is required in most states. In addition, there are certain courses which each state department of education specifies.

A school psychologist is in a strategic position. He

103

works closely with pupils, teachers and parents. Perhaps God would have you enter this great profession.

Government Service

"The penalty good men pay for indifference to public affairs is to be ruled by evil men."—Plato

1. *Why should evangelical Christians hold influential positions in government?*

America was founded by Christians on Christian principles. There is no better way to keep America strong than to have Christians in key governmental positions. Our government should be administered by Christians who will take their moral and ethical standards into government and help shape U.S. policies in accordance with a Christian philosophy of life.

2. *Is there a place in government service for well-trained evangelical Christian men and women?*

The United States government is not only wanting men; it is *hunting* for outstanding men who can serve in government employment. Apart from the military division, over two million four hundred thousand men and women are needed to serve all over the United States and in every recognized nation overseas.

3. *Where might Christians get college or advanced training for such positions?*

There are specialized schools that train men to enter diplomatic service and other specialized types of service.

However, government agencies specify that whereas they are hunting specialists in many professions, they can absorb hundreds of thousands of men and women who have college degrees with any broad coverage of arts, sciences or letters.

4. *Where can Christian young people get further information along this line?*

The Civil Service Commission in Washington, D.C.

is the main hiring agency for the U.S. Government. A book, "Federal Careers," is available through your local post office. It lists many hundreds of positions with the government.

Recently an influential man on Capitol Hill said, "We in Washington, D.C., are concerned over the lack of born-again Christians entering government service. We hope that every young person will seriously consider his place of service for the Lord. It may be in some influential branch of our government."

The Benefits and Liabilities of the Ministry

There is, of course, no greater or higher calling than the Gospel ministry. If you feel that God may possibly be speaking to your heart about the ministry, you will profit by considering this list of benefits and liabilities. It has been suggested by Dr. Russell V. DeLong:

1. A minister is responsible for witnessing and leading people to Christ.
2. He is accepted on the level of all the higher professions.
3. He is not bound by a time clock or ruled by a tyrant.
4. He is respected in the community.
5. He has an entree to nearly all organizations.
6. He can accept leadership in various benevolences.
7. His parsonage is usually free and sometimes furnished.
8. His utilities and care expenses are usually provided by his church.
9. His wife and children are welcomed and accepted in any strata of society.
10. The salary is small compared to that of other professions and vocations.
11. A minister is everyone's servant.
12. Often, he is subservient to people of lesser caliber and abilities.
13. He is restricted in his conduct and activity.

14. His hours have no time limit.
15. He carries everyone's burdens and sorrows.
16. He must be all things at all times to all sorts of people.
17. He must wear good clothes and be well-groomed.
18. He must keep up with new books and magazines.
19. His wife must be a model for the parish.
20. His children must be "perfect examples" for the children of his church members.
21. His own life should be the model of a good citizen, an ideal father, a perfect husband, a trusted friend and an exemplary Christian.
22. Unless he sets up careful safeguards, he has little private life.
23. He is frequently the object of criticism.
24. He is expected to be highly confidential.
25. He must receive his calling from God!

A Missionary for Christ

My mother used to tell me, "Son, the best things cost the most." Now I know what she meant. Service for God may be difficult but it also pays off in abundant joy.

A missionary calling is one of the highest. Its challenge is vividly portrayed in this poem:

Being a Missionary

Out where the loneliness presses around me,
    Looking on sights that are sordid and drear,
Strangely abiding—yet surely God called me,
    Why do I wonder if Jesus is here?

Strangeness of living and strangeness of people,
    Have I not come with the gospel of cheer?
Why is my heart then depressed with its burden?
    Isn't my Comrade—my Jesus, out here?

God! Teach me quickly to do without friendships,
    How to let go of those things that were dear,

How to be rid of this self that is binding me,
    Surely my Master, my Jesus, is here.

He, who is God, took the form of a servant,
    Humbled Himself unto death without fear;
Lonely, forsaken, despised, and rejected,
    My blessed Saviour, my Jesus, came here!

Wilt Thou forgive me for failure in serving;
    Heartache, depression, regrets, disappear.
Born of the Cross, a new courage infills me;
    Jesus, my Victory, my Life, is now here!

                                    —*Author Unknown*

Is God calling you to the mission field? If so, answer the call. You will never have peace and joy until you are obedient.

9

MILITARY SERVICE

FOR EVERY FELLOW . . . and for the girl in his life . . . military service looms with reality that can't be dodged. It's a part of our way of life, and it's here to stay.

Back in the twenties our fathers dreamed of a world without wars. But the world just isn't that way. The vast majority of the people of the world know not Christ as Savior. Many of them are at war with God and with their fellow men. On the other hand, there are many fine people, but without the restraining love of God in their lives they cannot possibly have peace.

You recall what our Savior said, "And ye shall hear of wars and rumours of wars: see that ye be not troubled: for all these things must come to pass, but the end is not yet. For nation shall rise against nation, and kingdom against kingdom" (Matt. 24:6, 7).

That's the picture of our world. *That's the way it really is.*

Add to this picture a shrunken globe that can be circled by giant jet bombers in a few hours, atomic and hydrogen warheads mounted on guided missiles, communist leaders making their plans for world conquest . . . and, well, that's enough. You see it. A nation like ours is a world leader and as citizens of a nation with international leadership we have no other choice than to play the role assigned to us. If we do not, we perish!

Although you can't side-step military life, you can take it out of the "necesary evil" category. Let's talk over some of the more important aspects of your place in military service.

It's an Honor and Duty to Serve

Serving our country can be a pretty impersonal affair. It's easy to say it's an honor, but not always easy to believe it. Not many fellows would argue that it's an honor to play on a nationally rated football team in a classic such as the Rose Bowl . . . or the Sugar Bowl . . . or the Orange Bowl. There's no question that this is an honor. A football game is something cut down to our size. But our nation—its very bigness makes for fuzzy, distant thinking. But for all its bigness it is no less real than the little things of football.

An honor to serve? Yes! An honor as great as the nation. Think what this means.

It means our homes, our churches, our schools. And it means our political liberty, too. Unlike many nations, we can work as we choose, travel as we choose, vote as we choose. It was Daniel Webster who said, "God grants liberty only to those who love it and are always willing to guard and defend it."

"Give me liberty or give me death" is no empty phrase. Down in your heart, these are your words, they are you.

But what about the Bible? It says, "Thou shalt not kill." And military service sometimes means war. And war means killing my fellow man.

I know. For some it is no problem. For others it is a struggle that tears cruelly at the center of life. You may recall the story of the Quaker family in that fascinating historical novel, *Friendly Persuasion*. A civil war. The call to protect country and home and church. But in these devout Quaker hearts there raged a war more terrible than that between the States. These Quakers, and others of like beliefs today, were not and are not cowards. They fear not death. They honor country and home and church. They simply do not . . . will not . . . kill a fellow human even if it means disobeying governments.

Let us not be hasty to criticize honest men whose conscience leads them this way. But by the large the Christian has through the centuries interpreted God's Word to mean that man as an individual or as part of a lawless mob shall not kill. But as a good citizen he is to obey the duly constituted government . . . even to taking up arms. Call to mind First Peter 2:13-15, 17: "Submit yourselves to every ordinance of man for the Lord's sake; whether it be to the king, as supreme; Or unto governors, as unto them that are sent by him for the punishment of evildoers, and for the praise of them that do well. For so is the will of God, that with well doing ye may put to silence the ignorance of foolish men: Honour all men. Love the brotherhood. Fear God. Honour the king."

Human government, even though poorly administered by man, is God's divine plan and purpose. The

Bible says, "The powers that be are ordained of God" (Rom. 13:1).

It's a Joy to Serve

Happiness does not depend upon *where* you are but *what* you are.

This is important. And especially important in the service. If you aren't happy in the service then it's more than likely that you won't be happy in other areas of life either.

I'll never forget the day I entered the service.

We were a motley crew. You would never think that a few minutes later we would all be officially inducted into Uncle Sam's Army, Navy, Marines, or Air Force. Some of the men wore suits. Others were dressed in loud sport jackets. And a few had levis with ten gallon hats!

After answering "here" to a muster list, we were lined up and pushed through a long barracks building. Down the center of the room was a string of tables with military personnel seated behind them. Every few feet they seemed to take our finger prints and ask us to sign seven more copies of one thing or another. In less than half an hour we were "processed." When I reached the end of the line, a fellow shoved a card under my nose and said, "Mac, this is your number: N326-475-927. Don't forget it, and don't lose it! You're in the Navy now."

About half a dozen self-appointed songsters chirped up and started singing — "You're in the Navy now, You're in the Navy now."

I thought to myself, *What am I doing in this outfit? I don't want to kill anybody. It sure won't do me any good, and I'll just waste a lot of valuable time.*

That's how I began my term of duty for Uncle Sam during the last World War.

But I soon learned that I had to take life as it came and make the most of it—no matter what my surroundings were. Sure, there were a lot of inconveniences in

111

the service. But there also was a long list of practical benefits. It didn't take long to find out what some of these advantages were.

In less than twelve hours after I joined the Navy we were on a troop train heading for a training center.

After they assigned me an individual roomette, I looked around and thought to myself, "Not bad, not bad. I couldn't even afford this as a civilian."

Then I settled down in a comfortable chair and began reading my Bible. After about ten minutes I looked up and wondered if someone might be phoning me. But in a flash I realized that I was no longer a civilian. *No one but Uncle Sam,* I thought, *needs my services, and he'll call me when he wants me.* So I settled back in the chair and continued to read. After another thirty minutes I instinctively looked around and wondered again if someone needed me or if there might be a phone call. But I again realized that I was no longer a civilian.

Suddenly the thought came, *It's been a long time since I've sat down and studied the Bible for forty minutes without someone interrupting me.* It was a new, yet strange and wonderful experience.

During the next few days I came to realize that in civilian life I hadn't spent much time in the Word. And I hadn't spent much time alone on my knees. But my time with the Lord on the troop train really paid off. How? During the first week in camp the Lord gave me the opportunity to organize a little Bible study group. And before the week was over, a dozen of the men in the outfit had given their hearts to the Lord Jesus Christ!

You may find the same thing when you serve Uncle Sam. You'll undoubtedly have much more time for Bible study and prayer. And if you're faithful to Him, He'll build you up spiritually and make you a stronger Christian — something that will serve you well all through life.

But there are many other advantages, too. Outside

of battle conditions you'll have a regulated routine of sleep, work, relaxation, exercise and study. Such a routine will tone up your muscles and give you a physical fitness that's next to impossible to develop in civilian life. And through this routine you'll learn discipline and co-operation — two fine characteristics that you'll always be thankful for.

Military training—yes! But your study need not be *limited* to military science. While you are in the service you'll have excellent opportunities to take college correspondence courses for full credit. Nearly every place you go you'll have a chance to attend lectures, visit museums and in general broaden your educational horizons.

Undoubtedly one of the greatest educational benefits results from the opportunity to go new places and see many things of real interest. During one year's time while I was in the New York City area, I took some week-end "liberties" to visit various universities. I saw Columbia, Harvard, Yale, Princeton and the University of Pennsylvania. I looked around—tried to feel the atmosphere of these great institutions. I talked with various administrative officers there and took their college catalogs. Interestingly enough, a few years later I enrolled in one of these schools—Columbia, where I received my doctorate.

When you stay true to the Lord, your spiritual development will amaze you. I speak for myself and thousands of other ex-servicemen who found an almost unlimited field for Christian contacts and witness in the service. And to the Christian, witnessing for Christ is one of the greatest joys of life.

It's a real thrill to remember the time that I was quartered in a Quonset hut not far from the Arctic Circle—in Iceland. We were stationed at the nation's capital, Reykjavik. Several young Filipino men had been shipped to Iceland to serve as cooks and steward's mates. One of them, Ben, was assigned to care for my quarters. I liked Ben from the very first morning that he came over to my quarters and started cleaning up. I thought to myself, "It isn't happenstance that God has moved a man all the way from the Philippines to Iceland simply to clean my room." I knew that I was there to witness, and I knew that Ben was there to receive the Gospel. So I prayed definitely that God would guide me in leading this young man to a saving knowledge of the Lord Jesus Christ. On the second morning when Ben came over to clean my room I waited there for a few minutes so that I might have a chance to witness to him.

"Well, Ben," I said, "how do you like Iceland?"

"It's okay, sir, but it's very cold, sir."

"How long are you going to stay in the Navy?"

"Oh, just two years, sir."

"And what then?"

Looking up from a bucket where he had been squeezing out a wet mop, his big brown eyes sparkling, he said, "Sir, I don't know just what I would like to do, but this I do know, I would like to be an eloquent speaker."

I smiled to myself and thought, *Here's my cue!*

"Well, maybe I can help you," I told him.

"Oh," said Ben as he stood erect, "I would be very happy."

I then explained to him that the greatest literature in all the world was the Holy Bible. I told him that if he would memorize portions of it I would hear him recite it each day and I would give him some pointers on "eloquent speaking."

Ben seemed to like both the idea and the friendship. The next morning when he came, he had the first Psalm memorized. He recited it in his broken English and then said, "But, sir, there's one thing I don't know."

"What's that?"

"The *righteous* man and the unrighteous man. I don't know who they are."

"Well, Ben, the righteous man is the man who is

114

right with God, the man who has given his life to the Lord Jesus Christ. But the unrighteous man is the one who thinks he doesn't need Christ and he has never given his heart to the Savior."

"Will you please explain again?" Ben asked. "I don't yet understand."

This gave me a real opportunity to talk with Ben about his soul. A few minutes later when I left the room Ben was standing by the desk — his left hand pointing to a verse in the Bible, and his right hand slowly moving a dust cloth over the top of the desk.

The next morning Ben knocked energetically at the door, then burst into the room saying, "I am saved, sir, I am saved!"

"Really?"

"Yes, sir, last night about midnight I began to think about it and I decided I was the unrighteous man so I got out of my bunk. I hit the deck and I talked to the Lord, and He changed me from an unrighteous man to a righteous man—now I am saved!"

And Ben *was* saved. As he studied the Scriptures and prayed, he grew into a stalwart Christian. In fact he was a remarkable witness there in Iceland—not only to the men on the base but to the Icelanders as well.

Conversions like Ben's are not unusual. Many men have been won to Christ through their buddies.

I recall a Sgt. Hill, who, while overseas, started a mission in a city of eighty thousand where there was no gospel witness. The mission grew steadily until it became a strong indigenous church! At the army base Sgt. Hill's witness was so clear-cut that many of his buddies later went into full-time Christian service.

With this list of practical benefits you can see how military service can be a real joy. And as you explore the opportunities you'll think of many other benefits— an opportunity to save some money, a chance to travel and be on your own, a chance to develop your personality by working with others.

You see the possibilities. It's up to you!

When Should I Go Into the Service?

The best advice anyone can give you about when to go into the service is this: *Build your plans around God, not the draft.*

Let me give you an example. Bill Wade was eighteen. He was a believer, although a fairly new one. He had a good high school record and lots of friends. His plans were for college in the Fall. But in July his best friend got the bug to join the Marines. So Bill got to thinking about the service and figured things out along this line: "If I join now I can forget about the draft and get my military service over with. And I can go in with my best pal. It'll be like old times."

So Bill enlisted. But his plan backfired. He was sent to South Carolina for training and his friend was sent to California. They never saw each other the entire time they served Uncle Sam. When Bill got out of the service he was a Private First Class. He'd lost most of his interest in going to church. His one desire now was to get any kind of a job that paid well. And he didn't think he had time to "waste" on college.

"But this is just one isolated case," you may say.

One case, yes! But not isolated. We see it happen all too often.

So you see, it's far better to go right on with life *until* the draft interrupts. Get as much Bible school or college training as you can. Then you'll be more mature and far better equipped to face military life.

Let's be realistic. You're going to hit head-on into man-size temptations, assignments and spiritual opportunities. Give yourself a fighting chance. Be prepared.

Marriage Plans and Military Service

An age-old, and frankly delightful, equation is: Boy plus girl plus romance equals marriage. Or at least it equals thoughts of marriage.

When a fellow goes into the service, the pressures

116

of sex and loneliness can become increasingly real to both him and the girl back home.

These pressures *could* be relieved by marriage. But a military marriage can have some mighty cruel pressures of its own.

Although one of your desires to get married may be a healthy sexual attraction, you know there is something deeper. You have a mutual respect and concern and sense of responsibility for each other. You know that marriage is a companionship in which each gives himself unreservedly to the other. But military life usually means long periods of separation. So you find yourself with more frustration than ever.

The first year or two of marriage demand many adjustments. But military life merely adds an additional adjustment. Too, a young couple needs a secure dwelling place with pleasant surroundings, near friends and church. These are seldom available in the service.

In a Christian marriage the husband has special responsibilities as the head of the home. But in the service he has about as much control over his decisions as a puppet.

And often there are more than just two people involved. Take the case of Glen and Betty. They got married just before he was drafted and she went to-be with him after he finished his basic training. On Glen's small salary they just barely existed, living in a pint-size apartment, eating inadequate food, and soon becoming dissatisfied, even with each other. After their baby was born, the picture was no better. Now the baby had to "scrimp" along with them.

Most fellows want to give the girl they love a chance to become a real individual in her own right before marriage. By remaining single while the one she loves is in the service, a girl can study, develop her talents—and in so doing be a far more interesting person when she marries.

Some fear a cooling of interest because of a long military separation. Sometimes this happens. But when it does, it's probably because the boy and girl were *wrong* for each other in the first place. And, in that case, it's a solid blessing that they waited to find it out.

Remember too that military life can change a man. Unless he grows spiritually while he wears the uniform, he may be quite different by the time he takes it off. These years of his life will greatly determine the kind of adult he will be.

Then, too, it's hard for a fellow to predict how he will feel about a binding thing like marriage—especially after having been marched, cooped up, yelled at, in combat and generally pushed around for several years.

All of this brings us down to a rather basic fact: *Military life is not conducive to building a happy marriage.*

But in spite of this, we realize that "good" or "bad" marriages are not made "in" or "out" of military service. They depend upon the maturity and spirituality of the partners and the Lord's will for their lives.

So in each case, the advantages and disadvantages must be considered and then the partners must be willing to follow God's guidance. "Delight thyself also in the Lord; and He shall give thee the desires of thine heart. Commit thy way unto the Lord; trust also in Him; and He shall bring it to pass" (Ps. 37:4, 5).

Which Branch of Service?

Regulations change from time to time, but a fellow can often select his branch of service. This choice should be made in the same way one arrives at other important decisions in life: Look to God for guidance, look to circumstances, look to your physical and mental aptitudes.

Some will like to sail the seven seas, some will like to burst through the sound barrier in a shrieking jet, some will like the wide variety offered by the army, and some will like the harsh, proud tradition of the Marines. Each branch offers its own particular types of specialized training; each offers a wide-open opportunity for Christian witness. Whenever possible select the kind of training that will further your overall life program. Being a radar repairman won't help you much if your life goal is teaching. In this case, it would stand you in much better stead to get something in the line of leadership or a personnel job where you'll be working daily with people.

If you, a Christian, have musical and clerical talent, one of the best jobs might be a chaplain's assistant. While some chaplains are godly men, there are those who evidently do not know the Lord. A born-again Christian assistant will have a real responsibility and opportunity to give a clear-cut gospel witness to the men in the unit.

For up-to-date information about the length of service and various training programs it is best to contact your nearest recruiting office or your local postmaster.

Officer's Training

For the right man, there are a good many advantages in taking officer's candidate training. You'll be trained for positions of influence and leadership. And you'll be associating with other competent young men with like aptitudes and ambitions. Many have found that after discharge from the service, their officer's training was a real asset in getting them better jobs with substantially more pay.

Of course there are determining factors. You have to pass rigid physical and mental tests and usually your length of service is longer if you become an officer. After you're in the service, your commanding officer will tell you (if you ask) whether or not you can qualify for officer's training. The final and most important of the determining factors is your desire for leadership. If you are not interested in assuming the responsibilities of leadership, then don't apply for officer's training. You'll be a misfit.

Attitude and Conduct While in the Service

Your attitude can make or break you in the service.

I mean it.

From the day you shed civilian clothes to the day you are discharged from the service you can either cooperate and expect no favors, or you can feel sorry for yourself, whine and be an all-around "goof-off."

I've seen ex-lawyers pull K.P. or clean washrooms all day. And they expected it. Naturally they didn't like it, but they didn't let it get them down. It was all a part of group discipline.

If you get started on the right foot, all of your service life will easily fall into order. And aside from the right attitude about military routine and discipline, there's your attitude about your Christian conduct and witness.

Spiritual Development and Responsibility

Your greatest personal responsibility while you are in the service (or any time) is your own spiritual life. But when you are in a definitely non-Christian environment, you must increase your Bible reading, prayer life and personal witnessing. When you find your soul dry and thirsty, claim a promise like Isaiah 58:11: "And the Lord shall guide thee continually, and satisfy thy soul in drought, and make fat thy bones: and thou shalt be like a watered garden, and like a spring of water, whose waters fail not." And then launch out. God always keeps His promise—even when you're in the service.

There is no substitute for Bible reading. To neglect it is to invite a fatal blow to your spiritual life. There is also a definite place for good Christian literature. Keep up on the latest Christian publications, tracts and books. (If there isn't a Christian bookstore near you, write to one.) Organize a Bible study class on your base. Participate in Christian service centers and organizations like the Navigators. All these things will help you grow into a stronger Christian and will make you a blessing wherever you may go.

120

Discharge

It was a "big day" for me—that day I took off my Navy uniform and entered into civilian life again. What a contrast to the day when I was inducted into the service. As I shed the uniform and dressed up in "strange" civilian clothes, my mind quickly reviewed the four and one-half years I spent in the service—and I found that they really were wonderful years.

Then in my room I knelt down by my bed and had a little talk with the Lord. I thanked Him for years in which I had grown spiritually; years that had given me many opportunities for soul winning. I praised God for His care over me, for the many times when He was so near and so precious to me. I praised Him for all of the wonderful friends I had made during the service. I thanked Him for permitting me to go to many interesting places and to gain a practical education. I thanked Him for the discipline and the hard work which came at times.

And then I asked the Lord to help me be as happy and useful in civilian life as I had been during the four and a half years that I had served Uncle Sam.

Happy in the service? Yes, I was. And many young fellows have had the same experience. They found that their years in the service became years of blessing and fruitfulness—not just "wasted time."

But it's up to you—and your willingness to obey the King of kings. When you serve in the armed forces of your country, you are a *Christian soldier* as well.

Yes, service life can be opportunity or temptation. It can be success or failure. So face it like a man . . . like a humble, Christian man, realizing that without His divine orders you cannot possibly win.

But with God's help (and it's yours for the asking), these can be wonderful years of your life!

10

DATING

STAN AND CHERYL were comfortably seated across from each other at the linen-covered table in the gracious setting of the Candelite Restaurant. As their eyes met, Stan's face lit up in a smile. *My,* he thought, *she's pretty and she's sweet! I'll have to make it a point to date her some more.*

As Cheryl returned the smile, she was thinking, *Stan sure is a swell guy. I hope he'll ask me again.*

Dating! A delightfully exciting kind of fun. It's the opportunity for fellows and girls to get to know each other as good friends and nice company. And maybe later on, even more than that. Who knows?

So, you see, it's important—*very* important!

Important that you have the *right kind* of dates—with the *right people*—at the *right times*—in the *right places*. These are the necessary prerequisites for having a good time. And when you disregard one or more of these *right* things in dating, you're liable to find yourself in hot water. When that happens, dates aren't so much fun.

Darlene found that out. She was as happy as a lark when Bob called for her Saturday evening. She had been "dying" for him to ask her for a date. Then one day he did. And now the big moment had come!

But Bob was not a Christian. And the evening wasn't the kind that Darlene had anticipated.

When Bob brought her home it was almost one o'clock. Darlene's anxious mother met her inside the door.

"You're awfully late, Darlene.'

"I know it."

"Anything happen?"

"No, nothing."

"Did you have a good time?"

"Oh, I don't know."

Then tossing her coat and pocketbook on the sofa, Darlene sank down beside them.

"Phooey," she mumbled, "I'm disgusted."

"Why, darling, what's the matter?" asked Mother. "Didn't Bob treat you right?"

"I didn't think he would be like that," Darlene answered. "He was fresh, and I justed hated him for it."

Darlene learned something from her date that night. She found out that sometimes it is better to stay home. And she discovered that it pays to *date right*.

Remember, *right* dating provides the kind of fun that will help you develop into a finer person.. And it's what you're looking for.

What Will Dating Do for You?

"Have you noticed the change that's come over Wayne lately?" Mother asked Dad.

"For the better or for the worse?" Dad teased as he looked up from the evening paper. He already knew in which direction the change had taken place.

"Why, for the better, of course," assured Mother. "He takes more interest in his appearance, even looks neat part of the time — and his personality seems to have just blossomed forth. Remember how bashful he always acted when people were around—but now he seems so much more confident."

"Yes," Dad joined in, "Wayne *is* improving in his social poise and growing spiritually, too — especially since he's discovered that those girls at church are *pretty important*. Where did you say he went tonight?"

"Oh, he went to a Youth Rally with Shirley," Mother laughed. "But these dates are doing him a lot of good."

And dates *are good* for people. Yes, here's something that's not only worlds of fun—something really exciting—but something that will help you develop as a more interesting person. That's why dates, the *right kind* of dates, are so important.

You can learn as much through dating as you can by taking a course in college. Through dating you learn your way around in a complex, social world.

When you date, you learn how you will react under many different circumstances. You discover your own strengths and weaknesses — and it helps you learn to get along with people. As you get acquainted with other young folks your interests in life will increase and you will develop socially. The more social ability you have, the better your chances of finding "Mr." or "Miss Right." And that's one outcome of dating—an important outcome—that of getting to know one person especially well, well enough to know whether you might like to marry him (or her).

But all this forms a strong reason for *not* going steady before you are ready. Sometimes going steady seems like an easy way out — but it may not be the real answer to your problem.

You may feel that by linking yourself up with one person, you secure for yourself a dependable date.

Perhaps you do — but unfortunately it may become *too* dependable! In other words, if you should try to break off, you may find yourself in an extremely difficult position. There are tears and misunderstandings. And embarrassment. Yes, someone is bound to get hurt.

Just because "everybody's doing it" in your crowd is an illogical reason for you to go steady. Going steady should be more meaningful than that. Usually young people who are going steady have some serious thoughts about each other. And if you have no intention of getting serious with your steady, it is unfair and unethical to string him (or her) along.

So go easy—and don't get too tied up with a steady before you are ready. If you do, you may lose out on a chance to date someone you would like much better. On the other hand, when you take your time and don't get too involved by going steady too soon, you'll have opportunities to meet many wonderful Christian young people. And when you do decide on a steady, it will be from choice and not from circumstance.

What Does It Take to Rate a Date?

Sue and Carol were roommates, and the best of friends. But tonight as Carol sat on the edge of her bed and watched Sue tripping gaily around the room getting ready for her date, she thought, *A date again! Sue has more dates than she can manage and I never have any.*

Carol felt a little pang of jealousy—and it made her ashamed because she thought a lot of Sue. But yet, to Carol it just didn't add up. "How come some girls don't seem to have any trouble getting dates—while others seldom get asked?"

Perhaps Sue and Carol had never analyzed what made the difference between them—but the boys who thought about dating them did. True, Sue and Carol were both sweet Christian girls, and perhaps Carol was just as nice to know as Sue—*when you got to know her*.

But most of the fellows weren't *interested* in getting to know her. In fact, they didn't even seem to realize that Carol existed. Oh, it wasn't that she was bad looking or anything like that. In fact, her features were basically more regular than Sue's.

So just what does make the difference? Perhaps this list would have helped Carol solve her problem: What does it take to rate a date? And maybe it will help you, too:

1. *Are you interesting?*

Can you *do* anything? Can you swim, or ride horseback, or play an instrument, or even bake a cake?

Do you know anything? Are you well versed in what's going on? Can you talk about things intelligently?

No one wants to date a *bore*.

2. *Are you vital?*

Are you alive and alert? Be a vivacious participant and you will not be a non-entity.

Does your personality sparkle? And are you generous with your smiles?

Remember, a magnetic personality will attract both fellows and girls.

3. *Do you look right?*

Do you do the best you can for yourself? Are you always clean and neat, and appropriately dressed? Do your clothes look "sharp," modern and well-fitted? And is your hair style right for you?

You don't have to be good looking to make a good appearance. And since a nice appearance plays a big part in getting you a date, don't ignore it!

4. *Are you good-natured?*

Can you *take it?* Do you join in the fun when *you* are the target of teasing.

Do you have a generous attitude toward other people? Boys don't like girls who are "catty" or "snippy."

5. *Do you have social poise?*

Do you know what and when to do and say? Do you know how to put the other person at ease—and be at ease yourself?

Do you act *yourself,* natural and relaxed? Christian fellows go for girls who are not "put on." So don't try to hard to "impress" them.

6. *Do you go to the right places?*

Do you go where there are good possibilities of meeting a dating prospect? You can't ask, but you *can* be available so when there's any asking done you'll have a good chance of being in on it.

But caution! Since you only want to date Christians *be sure you go to Christian places* where you'll meet other Christians. Church services, various church functions, youth rallies, outings, summer camps, Bible schools and Christian colleges—these, and many other places are good potential dating grounds.

7. *Are you too obvious?*

Are you trying too hard? You'll do much better to relax and not be so *over-anxious.* Of course you'd like to date, but don't act as if your life depends on it.

Fellows don't like to feel that they are being chased. They want to date someone of their own choosing.

So be more subtle. If you set the stage right you'll more than likely be chosen.

8. *Do you play "hard-to-get?"*

Are you *too* independent? This sort of thing can be overdone, you know. And it makes you appear conceited.

Fellows don't want to ask if they think they will be turned down. So remember, keep your poise but show your pleasure.

9. *Are you discreet?*

Do you do and say things that are "out of order"? Do you talk indiscriminately about other dates you have had?

It pays to keep your dating reputation on a good par. The word gets around, you know. And fine Christian boys aren't so interested in dating you if you are "that sort of girl."

10. *Do you pray about it?*

Do you commit every detail of your life to the Lord? Yes, *even dating.*

The Lord knows whom you should date and when you should date him. If you do your part to make yourself a desirable dating partner, then leave the rest in the Lord's hands. His will is always best.

But it isn't only a girl who may find it hard to rate a date. Sometimes a fellow is just as bad off. The girls avoid him like poison, laugh behind his back, and dig up all the worn out excuses they can find so they won't have to date him.

When a fellow's having this kind of trouble he'd better take inventory of himself. Better check that list we gave the girls. Try turning the tables and apply that questionnaire to yourselves, fellows. You might find that the shoe fits — and maybe even pinches a little!

True, girls have to wait to be asked. But fellows have to be accepted.

So, either way, put your best foot forward—and go places with lots of dating fun.

Whom Would You Like to Date?

Someone who's pleasant, someone who's interesting, clean, personable, considerate — and someone who's *lots* of fun. You can make your own list.

These things are important, *very* important. You don't want to date someone who is a bore, or a loudmouth, or just plain rude — or who has some other

128

undesirable characteristic. When you have a date, you want it to be with someone whose company you will enjoy.

That a person be good company is essential if your date is going to be a success. But there's another requirement that's even more important. It should be number *one* on your qualification list:

Is the person you are dating a born-again Christian?

Mildred was a sweet Christian. She was a woman all her neighbors respected. Her life was one of quiet courage as she faced her daily grief with strength from the Lord. Harry, her unsaved husband, owned his own small business. But Harry made little profit because he drank continually. When he was home, he shouted at Mildred, complained about everything she did, and watched the crudest programs on television, encouraging the children to do the same.

The unfortunate part was that it had been so unnecessary for Mildred to get into this domestic mess. But she chose it. She had grown up in a Christian home—had accepted the Lord as her Savior when she was young. She knew that the Scriptures clearly stated, "Be ye not unequally yoked together with unbelievers" (2 Cor. 6:14). But during her late teens, much to her parents' dismay, her Sunday school teacher's disappointment and her pastor's warning, she started dating Harry. She resented their "interference.' "It's my own business," she insisted, "and I don't see why they make such a fuss over a few dates."

But it didn't end in a few dates. She dated Harry, yes—and in dating him she became heart-involved and ended by marrying into a life of unhappiness. And not only did she suffer, but her children suffered, too. They had no real home life—the father pulling in one direction and the mother in another. Through it all, Mildred had peace in her heart because she repented and turned to the Lord; but she had to live with a heartbreak.

And there was Steve who became an executive in a

Christian organization. He maintained a fine testimony. But his wife left him because his Christian stand "got on her nerves." Although he remained with the organization, he lived a lonesome life without the sweet benefits of a Christian home and an understanding wife.

Examples like these are what make us realize how essential it is to date only those who are "out and out" Christians.

Naturally, just because you date a person that *doesn't mean* you are necessarily going to *marry* him. And it doesn't mean that you have marriage in mind every time you go on a date.

And you shouldn't! That kind of an unnatural, unwholesome attitude would spoil everything. Dating should be fun—good times—enjoying the company of the opposite sex.

But it would be pure folly to overlook the relationship between dating and marriage. Nothing follows a more logical sequence than dating — love — and then marriage.

And that's the pitfall. Dating, a pitfall? Yes, a subtle one. I've seen it happen many times. A fellow or a girl dates someone who isn't a Christian.

"Oh, we're just friends, nothing more. Don't worry. I'm not going to marry him (or her)."

That's what they say—and that's what they *think* when they first begin to date. But it isn't long before their friendship becomes more involved—and they find they're *in love*. And then it's too late.

And it all started with a few innocent dates—with the *wrong person*.

Should You Accept That Date?

"But can't I witness to someone who isn't a Christian by dating him?" you may ask.

It's dangerous. Because all too often the temptation to compromise will suggest itself. He may say, "Come to the dance with me Saturday night and I'll go to church with you Sunday." But bargaining is not built upon respect. Since no one wants to be a loser, it's only logical that a person won't try to bargain unless he feels fairly certain that he'll come out on the best end. And to bargain about right and wrong isn't even ethical — to say nothing of not being *Christian*. As one person put it: *"Doing wrong, to get a person to do right, is wrong!"*

Janet wondered about this. So one day she came to her youth counselor at church and asked, "Should a girl accept a date that will take her into a non-Christian environment?"

As the counselor talked with her he explained that God commands us not to participate in anything that might lead us into questionable activities. "Abstain from all appearance of evil" (1 Thess. 5:22).

"Janet," the counselor continued, "if you desire to follow the Lord, you shouldn't start out with the Devil's crowd. It's like this. If you are heading for a city in the north, why do you get on a train going south? Dates with unbelievers that take you to non-Christian places lead you in the wrong direction.

"Bill may not know any better than to ask you to go to non-Christian places. If so, this is your big chance to suggest that you go to a Christian place. This is one way you may be able to lead him to the Lord. And if he is already saved, you can invite him into a Christian atmosphere where he'll learn about living a consecrated life.

"If Bill really thinks much of you he will be happy to take you where you want to go. If not, he's not worth losing your testimony over!"

"Well then," Janet asked, "if I shouldn't go to these places with Bill, how do I refuse such a date?"

Janet asked a good question because she not only needed to know *what* to say, but *how* to say it. Her counselor gave her these suggestions:

1. If possible see him personally. If not, call him, or write him a note. But above all, be wholesome and forthright about it. Don't send word via one of

131

your mutual friends. Every boy admires a girl who is honest.

2. Start by telling him how much you appreciate the invitation. This will let him know that you are a fine, cultured person who genuinely appreciates invitations.

3. Next, tell him that although you *do* appreciate being invited, you feel that you would rather not go there. Then suggest that you attend a Christian function instead. (Naturally, it might not be on the same night, but that makes little difference.)

4. If Bill doesn't want to change his mind thank him anyway. Be sweet. Leave the way open for him to come to your Christian functions at another time. The Christlike *manner* in which you handle the answer is just as important as *what* you say. He will appreciate this courtesy from a Christian, and he may respond later on.

Where Do You Want to Go on a Date?

What is a date? Webster says (in addition to its other meanings), that a date is an *appointment* with someone.

So what is the thing that makes it really a date—the *person* you're with—or the *place* you go? It's *not* the place you go. You could go there by yourself, or with your sister or brother, and it wouldn't be a *date*.

So it *must* be the *person*. And it is. When you have a date with that pretty girl or good-looking fellow, it makes no difference if you step out for a "fancy" dinner or if you go for a walk. In either case, it's a date—because you had an "appointment" with him or her.

Naturally, the fact that you *go* somewhere or *do* something on a date is important, too. But not nearly as important as the person you are with. And because the one you are with often determines where you will go, it's all wrapped up together in one package—a date.

As a Christian, naturally you and your date will only want to go to places that are *right* for you. And you will not want to do anything that will impair your Christian testimony. No, of course you don't go on dates to night clubs, or dances, or other places that non-Christians think are so important, but you'll find plenty of other things to do and you'll have a much better time. (You might like to take a second look at chapter one for suggestions under the section, WHAT TO DO?)

So when you're deciding where to go or what to do on a date, ask yourself the question: "Does it glorify God?" This scripture is a guide to Christians in every area of living—and dating is no exception.

So—although going places and doing things are important in dating fun, it's not nearly as important as that interesting person you're with. You can have a good time *anywhere* if it's a place where you can glorify God.

What Is Your Courtesy Quotient?

If you are like about a million other young people, some teacher or counselor in high school or college has undoubtedly slipped up on your "blind side" and has given you an ability test. And about a day later he had your intelligence quotient tucked away in your records.

But has anyone ever figured out your *courtesy quotient?* It's important, too—in every area of life.

And dating is no exception. Check yourself on a few of these courtesies and see how you stack up:

1. *Are you definite when asking for a date?*

All too many fellows fall into the habit of pointedly asking, "Watcha doin' Friday night?"

Maybe the girl would like to go with him *some* places, but not any or *every* place. So, not knowing what he has in mind, she answers, "Plenty," meaning washing her hair (which she *could do* the next morning). So give her definite details, such as "How would you like to go to the class banquet with me two weeks from Friday?"

To that she can reply, "Thanks, Del, that sounds like fun. Can I let you know definitely tomorrow?" Then when she gives you her answer, you can make your plans.

2. *Girls, are you really honest?*

Fellows despise girls who lie to them. They don't mind being turned down or being only "one. of three boys friends," but they don't want to be lied to. That's something they can't excuse. So if you don't want to kill your popularity, you'd better not pull phoney excuses like, "I'm sorry, but I can't go with you tonight because I have to go to my uncle's funeral." It will be awfully embarrassing (and he'll be plenty mad) when he sees you at Funland with another date.

3. *Do you show the courtesies of calling for your date, exchanging greetings with her parents, then opening the car door and closing it?*

Even the president of the United States doesn't consider himself sufficiently important to merely honk to let people know he has arrived. Courtesies pay off in the long run because your stock will go up in the eyes of your date and in the eyes of her parents.

She may not be helpless, but, somehow for long centuries men have preferred to take care of ladies. It is their privilege. They let down the drawbridge over the moat. They held the horse's head while the lady mounted. And today a gentleman automatically opens the door of either the car or the helicopter. It takes only a few drops of courtesy to oil the hinges of life.

4. *Do you get the girl home at the agreed time?*

Parents feel that night, at least part of it, is for sleeping. Therefore, make a careful estimate of the time you have for the date—and having agreed to a certain hour, get her home on time, and with a smile. Then she'll be permitted to go out with you again.

Both she and her parents will have more confidence in you.

These courtesies — and others — can *make* you or *break* you as a desirable date. It's much more fun to date people who know how to act right. And a lot of people know the difference.

So fellows, don't be afraid to use your good manners. Be sure you carry her packages, and walk next to the curb, or push her chair in toward the table. Yes, that's it—treat the girl you're dating like a lady. She'll appreciate it—and other folks will respect you for it, too.

And girls, if it's his place to treat you like a lady, it's just as much yours to *act like one*. Give your date a chance to be a gentleman. Don't jump in and out of the car, slamming the door before he has a chance to do more than merely reach for the handle. And be sensitive to the amount his wallet can take. He'll appreciate your thoughtfulness.

Appreciation and respect. Yes, these are some of the benefits that will come your way when you are courteous and well-mannered on your dates. It pays in popularity!

What About Petting?

Not long ago I was leading a discussion with a group of young people when a fellow raised a question about petting. "Where does love end, and sin begin?" he asked. In other words, he wanted to know how much petting (if any) was O.K., and at what point petting would be so intense that it would be "sin."

Frankly, I was stumped for just a moment. But as I turned the question over in my mind, I realized that it didn't have a simple, one-sentence answer. It required discussion.

God has given each of us a capacity to love — to give and receive affection. When a fellow and a girl like each other a lot, it is only natural and right for them to express it. But it has to be within limits. This is God's plan.

The limits are lifted after they are married. Then, a husband and wife not only show their mutual love by their words and deeds, but also by the physical love which God has ordained for them. "Therefore shall a man leave his father and his mother, and shall cleave unto his wife: and they shall be one flesh" (Gen. 2: 24). Love-making in marriage is complete and it includes sexual intercourse. And it is love-making (kissing, caressing and other expressions of love) that prepares the husband and wife for sexual union.

Indeed, God has fashioned the human body and has given man and woman wholesome passions of sex. But with this endowment, He commands them *not* to engage in sexual relations outside of marriage. God warns, "Flee fornication. Every sin that a man doeth is without the body; but he that committeth fornication sinneth against his own body" (1 Cor. 6:18).

When a young man or woman understands that heavy petting is intended as a preparation for sexual relations, he can clearly see that outside of marriage it not only causes extreme frustration, but it also changes the divine purpose for which God has intended this kind of love-making.

Just recently a college student told me, "My sweetheart and I have a terrible problem on the weekends when I go home. We both become highly aroused. In fact we become so passionate that we almost lose all sense of right and wrong. Our relations have never been immoral. We love each other too much for that. We've talked it over but nothing seems to help. We won't be able to get married for at least another year. What can we do?"

This *is* a serious problem, but praise God, it has some common sense solutions! Actually, when they pet as they have been doing, they are engaging in God's intended preparation for sexual union. There is nothing wrong with their God-given passion. The wrong is this: Their petting is not rightly timed. It must wait until marriage. After they understand this basic fact, they will arrange to spend their time together doing a thousand other interesting things, and not permitting themselves to settle down by themselves in a secluded spot where they will stimulate each other in a sexual manner.

To what extent then, should those who are really in love express their affection for each other? The Word of God does not give specific answers to each couple. But it does declare, ". . . and whatsoever you do, do all to the glory of God." It is your responsibility to make sure that your conduct is honoring to Christ.

As a believer, you want God's best. You want it now and in the future. Every man respects a girl who is pure and wholesome. Every girl respects a fellow who is clean and manly. Don't fall into Satan's trap and sell your soul for a shameful experience that will haunt you as long as you live.

The most wonderful gift you can give your future bride or groom is your purity. When you walk down the aisle in marriage, you can look into each other's eyes and breathe a prayer of thanks that you belong to God and that He has kept you pure!

11

WEDDING BELLS

DEAN WATCHED ADMIRINGLY as Gloria walked grace-fully down the white carpeted aisle. *She's as beautiful as the bride herself,* he thought. Gloria noticed his approving glances, then smiled back.

Although Dean and Gloria were only the best man and the maid of honor, this wedding seemed more intimate than any they had taken part in. Was it the soft, golden glow of the candelabra, the beautiful, rich strains of the organ playing "I Love You Truly," the luxurious satin and lace of the swishy gowns, the gleaming white altar?

Partly.

But more than all the lovely, tender charm of the evening was the dream in their hearts that one day they too would be pledging their troth to each other— "Till death do thee part."

It's a rare young person indeed who can sit through a wedding ceremony and not dream. Just a little! You take it all in; you wonder about many things. You thrill with the frank joy of two people overwhelmed with love — two young lovers entering a delightfully mysterious experience together. And somehow, the anticipation is warm and wonderful in a way nothing else can be.

Nearly two hundred years ago William Cowper said:

> "Domestic Happiness, thou only bliss
> Of Paradise that hast survived the fall!"

But the blissful candles sometimes flicker out. Said a long-time married man recently, "Marriage is a mirage. When you look at it from a distance it seems wonderful, but when you actually experience it, you are disillusioned."

Brutally frank. But all too often tragically true.

You see, marriage isn't intended for everyone. Certainly it wasn't for the man who made that statement. And although some may think so, marriage isn't a cure-all for every unhappy person. In fact, usually when a maladjusted person gets married it results in two people being unhappy instead of one. And problems are increased rather than diminished.

So what about marriage? Is it delightful? Yes! Disillusioning? It can be! What it will be is determined by the partners. And by being in the will of God.

Marriage Is a Contract

Marriage is a contract. Sounds rather legalistic, doesn't it? And it is!

A contract may be defined as "An agreement between two or more parties for the doing or not doing of some definite thing; especially an agreement enforceable by law."

139

This doesn't sound romantic, does it?

But there is a God-given purpose behind the marriage contract. Young romantic love has a reckless abandon about it that is gay and dreamy and wonderfully sentimental. And it should be. But God has purposed that married love should develop into a family unit that is stable and Christ honoring. He has put His divine sanction and blessing upon the ordinance of marriage. And all those who enter into it are sacredly bound for life! "For this cause shall a man *leave* his father and mother; and *cleave* to his wife; And they twain shall be one flesh: so then they are no more twain, but one flesh. What therefore God hath joined together, let *not man* put asunder" (Mark 10: 7, 8, 9).

But just because there *is* such a contract, that doesn't mean the end of lighthearted romance. Actually the marriage contract gives a sweet stability to romance. And this is actually what every young fellow and girl wants.

Since contracts are binding we can't accept them lightly. Some young people spend more time and energy planning an educational program or a career than they do planning for marriage. This is wrong.

There are some girls (and fellows, too) who unthinkingly rush into marriage as a sort of solution to all their problems. I can't help but think of these young people as "distress merchandise."

Distress merchandise! (Cheap! Must sell within ten days!)

A cruel tag? It may sound that way, but it is true. And the consequences *are* cruel.

You know the type, don't you? Distress merchandise! Anything — anyone — just to get married. Oh, they wouldn't say it in so many words. But when you delve a little deeper into their motives—you find it's true. And it's an unsound basis upon which to build a good marriage.

Distress merchandise! But why?

For many reasons. It may be an unhappy home background, a feeling of inferiority, fear of loneliness, fear of financial insecurity, lack of parental training, a desire to escape school, sexual curiosity. And there are many other causes, too. But the most frequent type of distress merchandise that I find is made of girls who marry in order to get away from home. Girls who have a seriously unhappy home life should stop to think, then pray. They should never permit themselves to become distress merchandise on a cheap marriage market.

So when you start thinking about signing a marriage contract, think twice—or more. It's serious business. Marriage is a long-range relationship. Remember, you are saying "yes" for a lifetime. And it lasts throughout your twenties, your thirties, your forties, your fifties, your sixties, your seventies—yes, until death do you part! For something this permanent, take your time. Take weeks and months of thinking and praying and act only after you *know* that you are completely in the will of the Lord.

Fine print? Yes, most contracts have some. And the marriage contract does, too. This fine print is *extremely* important. So it pays to read it carefully. You'll find it contains instructions about such things as sickness, attitudes, mannerisms, financial reverses and values. Items that don't seem to be an issue before marriage, become *mighty important* later on.

And when you sign, there are usually some "extra" signers, too. Two sets of parents and other assorted relatives. Even if you may think so, your marriage is *not* completely your own business.

And relatives aren't the only "extra" signers. Believe it or not, employers are signers, too. Just before this book went to press, a friend of mine (a nationally known businessman) said, "How's your book coming along?"

"Fine."

"How about telling the young people something for me?"

"What is it?"

"Tell them that the person they marry seriously affects their employment. I never employ a man unless I know about his wife and family. I've learned from experience that a man with marriage problems always brings them to work with him. On the other hand, a man who is happily married always brings his happiness to work with him."

So be realistic and do some serious thinking *before* you sign. Ask yourself about the stability of your intended partner. And try to answer honestly. This isn't easy when you're in love. Right now you're living in a dream world that overlooks faults. But force yourself to be critical anyway. If you aren't before, you will be after you are married. And then it will be too late.

"How," you may ask, "can you tell if a person is stable?" There are a number of ways. Some of these suggestions may be helpful.

Try sitting down by yourself. Take a pencil and paper and jot down some known facts about the one you love. Be as detached as possible. Write down his or her *past* record for stability. Your check list will include such items as school, jobs, friends (of both sexes), church, family, goals, spiritual devotion. Ask these questions: Does his (or her) school record show that he sticks with one school of study? Does he have a certain type of vocation in view, or does he keep changing his mind? Does he attend one church for several years and enter wholeheartedly into its program? Does he keep his same Christian friends for a number of years? Does he consistently get along well with his parents? Answers to these questions will tell you whether he has much "stick-to-it-iveness"—whether he is stable, or whether he "shifts gears" too much.

If the list doesn't add up on the right side, go easy. Marriage *demands* stability.

142

The marriage contract presupposes certain responsibilities that absolutely require mature stability. For a woman it is the care of the home and of the family. For a man it is earning a living and protecting and leading the family. While both parents share in the training of the family, it is the man's duty and privilege to accept the responsibility as head of the home.

Home is a partnership. God expects the husband and wife to cooperate, to get their heads together and then come up with the best answer. But God *does* charge the husband with leadership. Girls, observe the Scriptures: "Wives, submit yourselves unto your own husbands, as unto the Lord. For the husband is the head of the wife, even as Christ is the head of the church: and he is saviour of the body" (Eph. 5:22, 23). And fellows, here's what God tells you: "Husbands, love your wives, even as Christ also loved the church, and gave himself for it" (Eph. 5:25). This is a tremendous command . . . *even as Christ also loved the church.*

Because this is true, no clear-thinking Christian fellow or girl is going to marry someone who isn't stable. A girl will only marry a mature Christian; one who can take his role as head of the home with a wonderful balance of respect and love and a deep sense of responsibility. And a fellow won't marry some baby doll who isn't willing to assume the responsibility of wife and mother. Both husband and wife have a definite role to assume—and it's all in the marriage contract. But these roles were never meant for children. That's why it takes mature people to bring about a happy, solid marriage.

But there's more to be considered than just stability and maturity when you are thinking about signing that all important marriage contract.

What about his religious faith? It isn't the same as yours? Oh, I know he may be handsome, kind, loving and have lots of ability. But it doesn't work. It's been tried thousands of times. And it won't work in your case, either.

It is often said that love is blind. And it certainly does seem to have some blind spots. John, for example, must have been blind when he went steady with Louise, a devout Catholic girl, and asked her to marry him.

Louise knew that her church would declare her marriage unlawful if she married a Protestant. She knew that according to her Catholic friends she would be living in sin and that their children would be illegitimate.

So Louise insisted that they would have to be married in a Catholic church. At first John thought this was a simple matter. But in time he learned that he would have to talk the matter over with the priest, then take a course of instruction in the teachings of the Catholic church.

Before marriage, he would be required to sign an agreement in the presence of the priest and two witnesses, pledging their intention to abide by the rules of the Catholic church concerning divorce, and that all their children must be baptized *only* in the Roman Catholic church and educated in the Catholic faith. John would have to promise that he would not interfere with his wife in her religion, and Louise would have to sign a separate agreement promising to seek to convert her husband to the Catholic faith.

Of course John had not bargained for all this. *He merely wanted to marry Louise.* But now he finds that he must sign a contract requiring him, if his wife should die first, to raise his children, his own flesh and blood, in a religion that he does not agree with, and a religion that will teach his children that John himself is a lost soul!

This is the price John will have to pay for not obeying God — for being "unequally yoked together" (2 Cor. 6:14).

The best way to avoid such a foolish and heartbreaking marriage mix-up is to avoid even entertaining the idea of marrying anyone of another faith. Not even dating such a person. It can *never* lead to happiness.

Finally — sign your marriage contract at church. Don't elope. Marriage is a Christian rite — so don't cheapen it by having a civil ceremony. Your marriage is so important and so sacred that it deserves a beautiful, sacred setting. Not only will it mean a lot to your family and your friends, but it will mean much to you and your mate as you look back and remember your wedding day. And when God gives you your own sons and daughters, they will ask you to tell them over and over again about your wedding!

Marriage Is Giving and Receiving Affection

Some young people think that love comes automatically through signing a marriage contract. But it doesn't work that way. Actually, some people aren't capable of loving anyone other than themselves. The solution to their problem is, of course, getting their minds off themselves and getting right with God.

And there are those who do love, but either they don't know how or they don't bother to show it. This kind usually comes from a home where love for one another was seldom shown. The first step to recovery comes when the person faces the facts and talks the situation over fully with someone he loves.

If you love someone enough to marry that person, show it. Tell it!

Love may seem like a spontaneous emotion. And in a sense, it is. But yet we know that love is something we learn—from our parents and from our friends. But what about those who are so unfortunate as to come from a home where love is never openly demonstrated? Can they learn to show affection? Yes, especially if they are Christians and learn the realization of Christ's great love for them. In order to be

145

happy — really happy, one must have the capacity to receive and give love.

The kind of love that makes a good marriage reveals itself in a hundred little ways. One has little concern for himself but is considerate and thoughtful about the other's needs and problems and desires. When we are thus concerned, each for the other, we automatically reap rich benefits ourselves.

And don't forget the *small* things. These are important in love. They set the stage for bigger things. It's this kind of consideration that becomes love in action—love that makes a marriage strong.

Since the love element is so vital in marriage, a great many young people ask me about love making before marriage. I've written a book, *Life and Love,* which covers this subject. But let's discuss it briefly here.

For the engaged couple looking forward to marriage it is perfectly normal for them to show their sincere affection for one another. But how about those unwise engaged couples who, to say the least, are not discreet? They go to an extreme in manifesting their affection. And by the time they reach the marriage altar they are little more than "technical virgins." Their conduct has been anything but Christ honoring.

The Christian solution—the one that Christ honors is this: Be affectionate to each other, but avoid affection which unduly stimulates you or your loved one sexually. If you "honor Christ in all things" He will truly honor you. It's worth it—well worth it, to have a pure conscience before God and the one you love— to do nothing that you'll ever regret or even blush over.

Use the engagement period as a delightful time to get to know each other better. But within definite Christ-centered limits. When you do this, it can be the most wonderful prelude to the physical joys that will begin after you have said "I do." Let nothing ruin these joys! To disregard God's commands brings shame and regret.

146

We hear a lot about physical incompatibility. But don't let it worry you. There is not much physical incompatibility among intelligent, healthy, mature, well-adjusted Christians. A few couples do have to seek counsel from a physician or marriage counselor, but this is the exception, not the rule. If you're basically happy, can give love, can receive love, are physically healthy and are more concerned about your partner's satisfaction than your own, you will have few problems with physical incompatibility that you cannot work out together.

Marriage Is Companionship

Recently I was talking with some young people about companionship in marriage. I emphasized the importance of *liking* (as well as loving) your intended mate so much that you can have worlds of fun simply being around each other. I assured them that there is the ecstasy of physical love. But for married people it is mostly "companioning." Going places together, doing things together, washing the dishes together, reading the paper together, riding to church together, talking together, working in the yard together, training and caring for the children together—just being companions.

And because this is true I always tell young people to make sure they can be happy just being good companions. *That's how you will spend most of your married life!*

Since marriage is a companionship it means that each partner will have to give up a lot of former independence. Dick and Joan found out about this. Dick was a champion skier.

Joan? She "hated" snow. Every time she got in it she had a severe sinus attack. Joan would have ended up a "ski widow" if Dick hadn't been willing to change his recreational pastime. But he did change. It wasn't easy, giving up the sport he loved so much. But he loved Joan more than he loved skiing. Together they turned to other things that they both could enjoy—

swimming and hiking. Does Dick still like skiing? Of course, but he rarely goes because he would rather be with Joan and he thinks too much of his marriage. When a fellow or a girl is not willing to sacrifice some activity or sport for the sake of his marriage, needless to say, that marriage is not going to thrive.

One of the hardest lessons most young couples have to learn is that marriage is *not* a 50-50 proposition! It is more like a 70-30 proposition, and *you* are the "30." If you go into marriage thinking you have the right to have your own way half of the time, your marriage will never be too happy. But it is the only path to follow if your marriage is to be a successful one. It works.

It means giving up many former relationships and developing new interests together. To do this you will need to be somewhat equal in interests, intelligence, education, social background and abilities.

I recently talked to a man who was having trouble because he and his wife were unequally yoked together intellectually. Both were Christians but she found him so dull that she became inwardly frustrated. He sensed it and tried to please her. The more dissatisfied she acted the harder the poor husband tried to please. They were getting nowhere fast.

He became her slave. Yet she didn't want a slave— but a partner.

They could have avoided this unhappy marriage if they had known each other better before they "tied the knot."

In education it isn't the years of formal schooling that always counts. Many folks are highly educated who have never finished high school. Warming a seat in college does not necesarily give you knowledge and education! It's what sinks in your head that makes the difference.

Companionship means walking together at the same time and at the same speed. For this reason it is extremely important that you marry someone from your

148

own culture and race. If you marry a person whose cultural and social background is dissimilar to yours, you'll find yourself in disagreement over *so many* details of life that you'll not be able to walk in the same direction, much less walk together. And your relatives won't help either. They'll be a constant source of irritation on both sides of the picture.

It is also highly important for the marriage partners to be somewhat equal in *energy output*. It is absolute folly for a ball-of-fire pace-setter to marry a languid snail-pacer. Each will be a constant irritation to the other. Opposites get along well? Don't you believe it! The more couples have in common, the happier they will be.

Marriage Is Earning a Living

There's a well-worn cliché that says, "Two can live as cheaply as one." Don't be fooled by it!

When a fellow marries he will increase his life insurance, his food bill, clothing expenses, utilities, medical bills and so on in almost every realm of living. Tom, for example, thought that two could live as cheaply as one, but after he was married a while and started paying the bills, he realized there were many extra expenses involved. In fact, he came to realize that two could live about as cheaply as *three!*

You may think that you won't mind scrimping along on a meager salary just so you can be married to the one you love. But too much of this (especially when it could have been avoided by waiting a little longer) can become pretty tiresome—and cause a lot of friction, too. That money is one of the main causes of marital disharmony is a proved fact.

So if you're wise, you'll check into your assets to see how well you can make it financially before you establish the business of "Mr. and Mrs. Incorporated." This means a secure job that provides an adequate income to meet your responsibilities in caring for a home and family.

Dave and Connie were having a rough time. They were married while he was still a junior in college. He had a good part time job and she was doing well as a secretary. They bought a G.I. home, furniture, and turned the old car in on a slightly newer one. A few months later Dave began to realize that they had bargained for more than they could cope with. Frankly, he was pretty worried about the bills. Their financial situation grew even worse when Connie had to stop working, and when the baby came. It's a matter of simple math.

You can't support a wife and baby and home and car on a part time job. So Dave had to drop out of college and start working in a gas station. That was four years ago. He's still pumping gas—afraid to step out and look around for something better because he's responsible for two other people besides himself. In Dave and Connie's case, marriage was not wrong, but it was *wrongly timed*. Because of this, their marriage got off to a wrong start. Financial problems have caused them much unhappiness, affecting their dispositions, their vocational goals, their sex life, and their spiritual development. And the lamentable fact is this —no doubt they could have been exceedingly happy if they had waited until they were vocationally and financially prepared.

Marriage Is Honoring and Serving Christ Together

There is no substitute for your own personal daily devotions. And marriage doesn't change this individual need. After you are married, both of you will still be individually responsible to God.

But there's more to it than that. When you become a family unit, you will need to have a daily *family altar*. The time of day you choose is not so important, but the fact that you have it every day is vital.

And when as husband and wife you worship together, you will find a holy oneness that is sweet and pure. Petty quarrels—problems—hardships—these will

150

all be taken care of in a miraculous way as you and your mate join hands around God's Word each day.

Close fellowship with the Lord is the "glue" that holds a marriage together. The reason why so many marriages fall apart is because there's no "spiritual glue" to bind them. Young people fall "desperately" in love, make promises, and show good intentions. But human love, promises and intentions can change to hate, accusations and self-will if the marriage partners are not saved, or if they are not having daily communion with God! Why is this? Because human nature is selfish and changeable. But the love of God is pure and entirely dependable. When a married partner is saved (has a new nature like unto God's) and when he is daily committing his life to Christ, his love becames pure and dependable.

In this age and society — when so many marriages are ending in divorce courts, "spiritual glue" is more important than ever. There can be no ultimate failure when a husband and a wife pray together about every problem that confronts them, every joy they share and every decision they make.

That is why it is dangerous business to marry someone who has not proved his Christianity. When you marry a person who was saved "just last Sunday" or "last month" you take a tremendous chance. Give him an opportunity to grow a little spiritually before you marry him — and a chance for you to know for sure that he really meant his decision.

And as for marrying someone who has been a Christian for years but who has never shown any signs of spiritual growth or maturity—better reconsider before you make a mistake. Such a person does not have enough spiritual glue to hold a marriage together. Sooner or later your marriage is likely to come apart. These people are serious risks until they become established in the Faith.

151

Marriage Is Establishing a Christian Family

It isn't always easy, this business of establishing a new family unit. I'm thinking of Ken, a godly young man who was deeply devoted to his mother.

Ken was president of his young people's society and his mother was a splendid Christian. But the day Ken married Lois some unhappy things began happening.

His mother asked the young couple to live with her, and they unwisely accepted her "generous" invitation. After all, it saved them money, and that's what they were especially short on. The mother continued to "help" Ken. And within two years Lois was ready to call it quits.

Undoubtedly Ken's mother was sincere and also good-hearted. But do you see what they had done? All three of them had disregarded God's command to *leave* and *cleave*. When a man and woman marry they should *leave* their families and *cleave* unto each other. That's God's way and it always works out best.

So when you get married, get away from your parents and let God establish your own home.

Thinking about establishing a Christian family usually involves children. The Bible says that "children are an heritage of the Lord" (Ps. 127:3).

And since children are a part of your future plans, you'll want a mate whose personality, health and intelligence are of the quality that you wish to give to your children. Remember, one-half of your children's basic qualities will come from your mate. When you choose your mate, you are affecting all of your children, grandchildren and great grandchildren!

Because children aren't "incidental" they require parents who have enough time, money and patience to care for them. Unless you are ready for a baby's cry, for hours of broken sleep at night, and for many other details that accompany a helpless infant, you had better let your marriage wait. God holds you responsible for the precious lives He gives you. And it's a tremendous challenge.

Yes, children are a part of the responsibility that comes with marriage — but they are more than that. They are one of the greatest pleasures ever given to a family.

Before You Say "I Do"

So—looking forward to marriage! What a thrilling subject to think about when you're young and alive with dreams of inviting experiences that wait just around the corner.

Young love is wonderful—warm and gay with rapture and mystery. It puts the stars in your eyes and the flutter in your heart.

But before you sign that marriage contract, try to set your feelings aside for awhile and carefully review the important things that make for a happy marriage.

You'll remember that marriage is not a cheap thing; it is a sacred lifetime contract—a Scriptural one as well as a legal one. It is a life commitment to be worked at for a lifetime. There can be no quitting, no turning back. So make up your mind that *your* marriage will be a success. And then approach it with that determination.

You'll not look for perfection. There is no such thing. But you will look for spiritual and emotional stability and maturity. You'll look for adequate, dependable earning power. You'll look for someone who not only can give and receive love but who can also be a companion day in and day out. For five, ten, twenty-five, for fifty years—"until death do us part."

And when you've finished your check-list, you'll know as you've never known before that marriage is not for children, but for mature grownups. And it's wonderful!

12

GOD'S WILL FOR YOUR LIFE

JOHN AND JOE TALKED and laughed as they strolled across the campus. They had been friends for several years, but recently, since they had both given their hearts to Christ, they had become even closer.

During their senior year in high school they had attended a week-end conference sponsored by their church. It was then that they surrendered their lives completely to the will of God.

A good start? Yes, it couldn't have been better!

Joe finished college, and although he didn't set any great records, he graduated with above average grades. Two years later he married a fine Christian girl, then entered full-time Christian work. Today, Joe and his family are exceedingly happy. And what a blessing they are to other people!

John? Well, he started to college, but he only lasted two years. After a year or so he got married. But that didn't last either. Right after his first baby was born he got a divorce. Then he knocked around for awhile —one job after another. Then he married again. And through the years John lost his sparkle. His dreams for the future left him. And today he has little effect on others—in fact, few people know he's around.

John's tragedy is what you want to avoid. God wants you to be successful. He intends that your life be packed with happiness and achievement. Christ Himself said, ". . . I am come that they [Christians] might have *life,* and that they might have it *more abundantly*" (John 10:10). What could be plainer?

Abundant life! It's what you and every other young person want—days and years that are bursting with good times and victory! But there's only one place where you can have this kind of life. Where? Right in the center of God's will. That's the *only* place of genuine blessing.

"Well," you say, "if God really has a place for me, I'd like to know what it is."

Yes, perhaps you (like many others) have been troubled by this big question: How CAN A PERSON KNOW GOD'S WILL FOR HIS LIFE?

You *can* know. Without any shadow of a doubt. And it's not guesswork. That would be dangerous.

Yes, there is an answer! God does not tease people in this matter. He has given a clear, simple, workable answer. And when you get it you'll have inward peace, top efficiency and maximum productivity.

But God does not, will not force you to follow His will. He does not coerce you or impose His plan upon you. The choice is yours! You are free to yield or reject. But this is certain: Any person who wants God's guidance and WHO SEEKS GOD'S WILL can count

155

on Divine direction. Nothing delights God more than to lead Christians in His own way—the very *best* way.

Reporting for Duty

The story is told about a soldier who was transferred to another assignment. After arriving at his new base he contacted his superior officer and told him about all the things he could do. After letting him talk for a few minutes, the officer said, "Private Smith, your only responsibility is to *report for duty.*"

If you truly want to know God's will for your life, you must begin by reporting for duty. God wants your availability. He wants you to be willing to do anything you are asked to do. He demands total dedication. And when you enlist, you are responding to a call from God.

It is not up to you to ask where you are to go, or how soon. But it is your responsibility to report for duty. Remember, you are not only volunteering, but God is calling you.

The psalmist had the right attitude when he said, "Cause me to hear thy loving kindness in the morning; for in thee do I trust: cause me to know the way wherein I should walk; for I lift up my soul unto thee" (Ps. 143:8).

You cannot be led unless you are *willing.* God attempting to lead a person who doesn't want to be led is like someone trying to lead a stubborn mule. What does the mule do? He sinks all four hoofs into the ground, then leans backward at a forty-five degree angle.

You get the picture. Rebellion, stubbornness. Some *people* are like that. They have their own plans in mind and don't want any interference from God. The last thing they want to do is to report for duty.

"But," you may wonder, "can God actually lead me?"

Yes, He can. And He *will* if you'll let Him. God gives us His gracious promise, "Trust in the LORD,

156

and do good; so shalt thou dwell in the land, and verily thou shalt be fed. Delight thyself also in the LORD; and he shall give thee the desires of thine heart. Commit thy way unto the LORD; trust also in him; and he shall bring it to pass" (Ps. 37:3-5).

I once knew a girl, Phyllis, who said that she would be glad to do anything that the Lord would call her to do, just as long as she had the opportunity to play her violin. Phyllis was an *excellent* violinist. God had given her unusual ability. But God did not call her. Why? Because her violin stood in the way of a one hundred percent committal. God isn't interested in volunteers for service who come with reservations. He wants our all. He wanted Phyllis to be *willing* to give up her violin.

But there's a happy ending to this story. In time Phyllis reached the point where she was willing to give up her instrument entirely if that was what God wanted—just so she could serve Him.

That was the beginning of finding God's will for her. He led Phyllis into a rich and useful life— and as one might expect, she also had many opportunities to play her violin!

There is little use for you to look for God's will for your life until you have given up completely. You must be willing to do absolutely anything that He might call you to do. It might be at any time, night or day, alone or in a church service. But when you're serving in the Lord's army you follow orders—seen or sealed.

Step by Step

Let's stop just long enough to be sure of one thing: If you want to know *all the details* for the next fifty years, if you want to see the road ahead to the end— around all the turns—over all the hills—through all the valleys, you're going to be disappointed. Because God doesn't work that way. It's not like a cut and dried blueprint or like a mold that had been cast. God's will is active, dynamic, immediate. Like *a potter shap-*

ing clay in his hands. It's a minute by minute, step by step process.

But the thing that you *must* know is that you are being led — moment by moment, step by step. God will establish your thoughts, order your steps and direct your paths. You may not know how God is leading BUT WE KNOW GOD LEADS! And that's all that really matters. God promises to guide us. "I will instruct thee and teach thee in the way which thou shalt go: I will guide thee with mine eye" (Ps. 32:8). And He is *absolutely trustworthy*. His word is His bond; He can be depended upon implicitly. We do not know the way BUT WE KNOW THE GUIDE and we have complete confidence in Him.

This is God's plan for every individual — for you! COMMIT YOUR LIFE TO HIM. Surrender to His will daily and ratify that surrender as often as necessary. When you yield to His will, He does the leading. He guarantees it!

There's nothing mysterious about the will of God. It's like taking a trip. Following God's way is an *exciting adventure*. Life is never so interesting as when one takes the will of God seriously and travels in that direction.

When a person begins a trip he is *sure of his destination*. But he is not familiar with every mile of the way. That would turn a trip into boredom. Usually he has a map which points out the way he should go— suggests some of the things he should see enroute. As the traveler journeys he sees as far ahead as the road permits. Sometimes it's many miles, sometimes but a few yards. A turn in the road, a hill, a clump of trees—any number of things may limit his view ahead.

But he doesn't get alarmed because he cannot see beyond the next curve or over the brow of the hill. He knows that when he goes as far as he can see ahead— a new view waits to be unfolded before him.

Knowing God's will is a daily experience of daily leading. His Word becomes "a lamp unto my feet, and a light unto my path" (Ps. 119:105), shining just far enough ahead that I need not become discouraged over the magnitude of the future.

Two things are imperative: First, keep on going even though you do not see very far ahead. Second, stick to the road. It was built to bring you to your destination. Obviously it won't do it if you refuse to stay on it.

This is life in the will of God! The destination is absolutely certain — heaven is the goal. Familiarity with every step of the way is unimportant. The Bible is the infallible map and guide. Jesus Christ is the road—the WAY!

The important thing is to *get on the road* — and *keep going.*

It is as foolish to get nervous and anxious when God does not reveal all the way ahead as it would be to become distracted simply because one cannot see the highway over the hill or around the corner. Imagine the traveler refusing to go forward until he could see the entire journey laid out before him. For example, some young people would like to take a journey through college but they never start the trip because they can't see more than a semester or two ahead. How foolish! What they *should* do is go as far as they can on the right road. Then God would show them a few more "semesters" of road.

Walking in the will of God as far as one can see, no matter how brief the view, will lead inevitably to new vistas, new heights, new beauty. Doing the thing at hand is the surest guarantee that there will be more to do.

Something more to be said: The traveler keeps his *destination* in mind. This helps him over the rough spots. Christians don't quit when the way is rough. Because they have their minds on the future just as much as they do on the present. AND THERE WILL BE ROUGH SPOTS. Sometimes there are detours. Often these detours lead to the most fascinating experiences

159

of the trip. Sometimes the traveler talks and laughs most about these when the trip is over. When we see them in their proper perspective they afford our greatest joy. How true it is that often our disappointments prove to be His-appointments.

So keep your eyes on Christ. Follow Him. And walk by faith—it's far better than sight. It's the life of adventure and joy—and accomplishment for God.

The Secret Place

This is an interesting fact: Christians who go on their knees go much faster. So if you want the most direct route to happiness, get on your knees before God.

God tells us in James 1:5-7, "If any of you lack wisdom, let him ask of God, that giveth to all men liberally and upbraideth not; and it shall be given him. But let him ask in faith, nothing wavering. For he that wavereth is like a wave of the sea driven with the wind and tossed. For let not that man think that he shall receive anything of the Lord."

Yes, "pray without ceasing" (1 Thess. 5:17). And pray fervently—and pray in faith believing that God will answer your prayer. Pray realizing that you, a Christian, belong to God's inner group, like the early disciples did. And when you pray, do it in the spirit of thankfulness. "In everything give thanks; for this is the *will of God* in Christ Jesus concerning you" (1 Thess. 5:18).

And be patient. God will reveal His will to you in His own time. But be sure you pray with an open heart — willing to accept the "no's" as well as the "yes's." And also the "wait awhile."

When you begin praying about God's will, you may find that you want your *own* will more than you want *His*. The best way to settle the issue is to go to your room or some place where you can be alone with God. Then talk to the Lord about it. Not only will God answer your prayer but as you talk over this problem

with God you will soon realize whether you are praying for your own wishes to be accomplished or "Thy
will be done."

A Lamp and a Light

There are "know how" books for almost everything.
Rules for playing tennis, recipes for baking cakes,
guides for banking, suggestions for parties—rules and
guides for almost every occasion. But the greatest
guide book in all the world is the Bible. If you really
want to know God's will for your life, devote yourself
daily to reading God's Word. It has the answers and
will help point the way for you. It is a *sure* guide.

Praying is "you speaking to God." But reading the
Bible is "God speaking to you."

The Bible gives people general and specific directions. In it we read about many Bible characters and
how God's will was wrought in their lives. Christ did
the will of the Father even unto the death of the Cross.

When you read the Bible, God will speak to you
personally through it. Believe it and appropriate it to
yourself. The path has been mapped out for you.
Follow the directions and you won't be confused.

Since the Bible is a lamp unto our feet and a light
unto our path, let's not hesitate to use it. We need the
lamp so that we can see step by step and we need the
light so that it will shine down the path a little way.
Naturally you cannot see all the way but you can see
enough to take the next step and keep on the right
path.

A light and a lamp! God's Word will be exactly
that. It is impossible to *know* God's will and to *stay*
in His will without reading the Word of God!

Now

Janice attended college in the city where she lived.
One day she was talking with her pastor about how she
might know God's will. He pointed out to Janice that

her first responsibility was to be faithful to the tasks at hand.

"For example," he said, "you are a good pianist and you should be faithful as a pianist for your young people's group. And Janice, you can distribute attractive tracts and witness to your classmates."

Janice thought it over. She began to realize that she hadn't been as faithful in these basic duties as she might have been.

"It's like starting from the beginning," mused Janice. She prayed that the Lord would help her—then she started in. Before long she found that she was doing these things with real satisfaction. She became faithful in her own church and in her Bible study, prayer, and witnessing. In short—God was leading her. This was her first effort to find God's will for her life.

As Janice continued to follow God by using the opportunities for service that were at hand, He led her into still other avenues of service. Today she is in a very responsible position—a truly happy person. Why? Because she was faithful to the "smaller" tasks. Since God found that He could trust her He continued to give her further responsibilities. And she was ready to take them. She had served her apprenticeship and had proved herself.

That's one of the ways—a very important way—to discover God's will for your life. When you are faithful in the little things, then God will lead you further. Yes, your present is determining your future. Use every present opportunity. This may be your tryout. Don't flunk! Your present service will open doors for the future.

But you are not likely to learn God's will for the *future* if you don't learn His will for *today*. The person who really wants to know God's will does the things he already knows about. When he does this, he makes himself available for opportunities—big opportunities.

As we study the Scriptures we find that there are

many things that all Christians should be doing every day. And there's no question about God's will in these matters. For example, in Acts 1:8 God tells us ". . . ye shall be witnesses unto me both in Jerusalem, and in all Judaea, and in Samaria, and unto the uttermost part of the earth." And again we read "The God of our fathers hath chosen thee that thou shouldest know *His will* . . . for thou shalt be His witness unto all men of what thou hast seen and heard" (Acts 22: 14, 15). The orders are plain. God commands us to witness.

One of the most important things in being in the will of God is to start with what you know. A stalled car cannot be driven. A ship in dry dock cannot be navigated. So *start* in the right direction and God will lead you the rest of the way.

You may not be certain what God has for you in the future but you certainly can know what He would have you to do today. How about teaching that Sunday school class? And assuming more responsibility in your youth group? Are you a member of a gospel team? Are you faithful in witnessing to others? Do you consistently have daily devotions?

When you learn to be faithful to the duties around you, in due time God will give you other responsibilities. He says ". . . because thou hast been faithful in a very little, have thou authority over ten cities" (Luke 19:17).

So be faithful to the tasks at hand!

Your Natural Endowment

I can still remember a certain classmate in college. She was a pleasant girl who played the piano. But she over-estimated her ability. Her ambition in life was to serve the Lord as a pianist for some evangelist. Actually, she had very little musical ability and her piano playing was mediocre. Fortunately, her piano teacher helped her to realize that she did not have enough talent to become a good pianist. Finally the girl reached the point where she was willing to give up this idea and prepare for a different field of service—one that would better suit her ability.

It's a smart person indeed who takes a good honest look at this talents. How much better it is to face facts and admit that you can't "cut it" than it is to become involved in a work in which you will be nothing but a failure. And it's not God's will that you should fail, but that you should succeed.

Is there a place, then, for ability and aptitude tests?

Yes, there is; a *very* important place. If you are in college or in a high school where it is possible to take tests, you should do so. Then talk with your counselor about your scores. This is one excellent way to learn about your potential abilities. And Christians can benefit from scientifically developed tests just as non-Christians can.

God may have given you certain abilities that you have never brought to the surface. Sometimes we are surprised at what we can do. This is even true of psychologists!

Not long ago I was talking with a pyschologist who had recently entered the profession. He told me that his great weakness was public speaking. He was afraid that he would never be able to command the attention of an audience. Yet, in his work it was imperative that he learn to speak to groups.

I suggested that he start working on it by listening to other people and finding out what made them effective as speakers. I suggested that he read several books on public speaking; then prepare outlines for several talks and accept a few engagements where he could speak to small groups. He tried it. It wasn't long until he was speaking quite well. You see, this man had the potential ability. But it had not come out before because he had never studied speaking and because he had never practiced it.

Yes, you may have more potential than you realize —and more than *other* people realize too.

I'm thinking of a missionary who was rejected by several mission boards because they felt that he didn't have enough ability to do the job. But he was certain that God had called him and he was determined to go. So he paid his own passage to Africa and supported himself on the field. It wasn't long until people (the mission boards included) recognized him as one of the most outstanding missionaries of his time. He had proved himself—and God!

No one has all the ability and personality he would like to have. And sometimes this is an advantage. It keeps a person more dependent on God!

No, you don't need "all of the ability in the world!" God will more than make up for it when you are doing His will. He tells us, "Fear thou not; for I am with thee; be not dismayed for I am thy God: I will strengthen thee; yea, *I will help thee:* yea, I will uphold thee with the right hand of my righteousness" (Isa. 41:10).

Words of Wisdom

Jack was doing a splendid job. He was young, earnest, talented—and he was using his abilities for God. But one day another Christian organization offered him a "better" position. It looked promising. Jack prayed about it but he wasn't sure that he should make the change. Finally he went to a friend who was an outstanding Christian leader and asked his advice.

"Listen, Jack," his friend said, "the job you now have presents much more opportunity for service than the one you are being offered. If you take the other job you will be stepping downward. You have a unique position—one which very few Christians are trained to fill. If I were you, I would stay where you are."

That settled it for Jack. As he went home and thought about it he realized that he should refuse the new offer. A few years later he saw that if he had changed jobs he would have made a big mistake.

165

The Bible teaches that "Where no counsel is, the people fall: But in the multitude of counselors there is safety" (Prov. 11:14). How true! Many young people have been helped to discover God's will by talking with godly men and women who have had a rich background of experience. Spiritual people of this caliber can give you the advantage of their own valuable experience. And often God speaks through them. They know the needs of the day and they can foresee many difficulties as well as many opportunities.

If you have earnestly sought God's will for your life but have not yet contacted some outstanding Christian men and women, try it. God may use them to speak to your heart.

But be careful *whose advice you seek*. Make sure it is someone who is in close fellowship with Christ.

Information Please

Someone has said, "There is no premium on ignorance."

How true! And as Christians we shouldn't be lacking in knowledge. We need to be well-informed about the needs of the world and the many places where we might serve. This knowledge can serve as one basis on which to make a decision as to the right place of service for God.

"But," you may ask, "doesn't God lead us into places of His choice?"

Yes, but He expects us to do our part. It's difficult to become interested in a field that we know little or nothing about. So it's up to us to learn all we can about various fields of service.

This is an interesting assignment. There are many sources of information available. If you are seeking to know God's will for your life try reading a number of Christian books, especially biographies. They may challenge you to serve God as a business man, a secretary, an educator, a psychologist, a missionary, a minister, a youth worker, or in some other field.

166

Another suggestion: Read Christian magazines each month. Through them you can know the thinking of many of our outstanding Christian leaders. And surely you will receive valuable guidance from their inspirational and Christ-centered writings. If you will allow time for reading Christian books and Christian magazines, God will show you many never-before-realized opportunities for service.

Another excellent source of information is Christian films. During recent years many challenging films have been produced. Some of them present the need for Christian workers in various fields and in different parts of the world. So view all the Christ-centered films that you can. The information that is brought to you through them may bring you the challenge you need.

If you attend a Christian college or a Bible institute, some of your courses may help you in finding God's will. These courses may be in journalism, sociology, missions, or in any other field. You can learn about the extensiveness of various professions and the opportunities to witness for Christ. If you are *not* in school you may find it helpful to take evening or Saturday courses in a nearby Bible school or Christian college—or perhaps a correspondence course. The knowledge gained and the inspiration received can help you immeasurably in knowing God's will for your life.

But if you *are* attending a Christian school you can also join the various campus organizations (education clubs, missionary groups, literary societies). They make it a point to find out the needs of various Christian enterprises today and they bring them to the attention of their members.

And what will all this information add up to? Just this: It will give you a better background. It will make you a well-informed person who knows what is expected (and what to expect) in various fields of service. And you will be more capable of discerning God's will for your life.

Urgency

Sometimes God calls a man for a specific job at a specific time. The call is urgent. It must be answered *soon*.

That's what happened in Gordon's life. He was a senior at a Christian college — an education major. One morning during the chapel service a returned missionary presented a stirring challenge. He told about the need for men in the field of education who would serve in a foreign land. The speaker was recruiting a few select men. As the missionary gave the challenge Gordon's heart was stirred. It seemed to him that no other message had ever burned so deeply into his heart as did this one.

After the service Gordon went to the front to meet the speaker. He arranged a time when he could talk with him about the challenge he had presented. The missionary suggested to Gordon that he could leave the United States soon after he graduated. Four months later Gordon was sailing across the deep Atlantic with his diploma in his suitcase. It wasn't long before he had real opportunities for service. As an educator in a foreign country he was respected. He made friends with the natives, thus giving him the opportunity to lead many of them to the Lord.

Gordon was happy. He was in the will of God. And he thanked the Lord many times for leading him to this field—and for the urgent call that God presented to him that day in chapel.

Are you looking for God's will in *your* life? Then listen carefully to every challenge you hear. Ask yourself, "Is this something for me to know about? Is this a challenge for me to consider? Or is it a definite call for me to heed?"

Urgent, specific calls not only come for foreign fields; they come also for avenues of service here in the homeland. So don't rule out the responsibilities nearby. Sometimes the greatest jobs are found close at hand.

A call from God is not based upon a *location* where you might serve. Rather, it is based upon being in His appointed place. "Thou wilt show *me* the path of life: *in thy presence* is fulness of joy; at thy right hand there are pleasures for evermore" (Ps. 16:11).

Your Responsibilities

Whenever I talk with a person about God's will for his life I always ask him what his present responsibilities are. Why? Because it establishes a starting place. God doesn't intend for us to disregard the responsibilities and duties which have already been placed in our pathway. Occasionally I meet someone who thinks he has a call for a certain type of work—but in reality it is only a human desire to dodge a responsibility he already has.

I knew of a Christian man and his wife who had seven children. The husband heard a stirring missionary challenge and "right then and there" he decided that God wanted him to leave the United States and go to a foreign field. He talked it over with his wife. But she did not share his vision. Although she prayed about it, still she didn't feel that she was called to go. But the husband insisted that she was "all wrong." Since she would not go, he decided to go to the mission field without her. "I'm going to follow God even if she doesn't," the husband persisted.

She remained firm in her stand. So he took the seven children with him to the foreign field and left his wife at home! The mission board then sent two missionary ladies to care for and to educate the seven children while the man did his missionary work. Foolish? Of course! The mission board did gain *one* missionary, but it lost two, those who had to take care of his children.

Furthermore, this man's first responsibility (since he was already married and had a family) was to care

169

for his wife and children. That is the clear, plain teaching of the Word of God. So he certainly could not have been in God's will.

Was his wife right or wrong? We do not know. But even if she was completely wrong, this still did not exempt him from his responsibilities as a husband and a father.

Responsibilities? Yes! But they are more than that. They are our God-given opportunities.

But let's consider another side to this question of one's present responsibilities. Merely because you have a job doesn't mean that you should stay in it forever. Sometimes God calls a person out of one job and leads him into another.

That's the way it was with Marian. She was a stenographer for a Christian organization. Using her life for the Lord? Yes. But one day she heard a challenge about a different type of work. Marian thought seriously about it but reasoned, "I'm working for the Lord where I am. Why should I move?"

After several months of deliberation Marian finally decided that although she had been in God's will, He was now leading her into another type of work. So she took additional training and accepted the new position. After she had been in the work a short time she could plainly see God's wisdom in directing her there. God had led her and she had peace and joy in her new field of service.

So take a look at the responsibilities which God has placed in your path. If you are thinking of going into a different type of work, seriously consider your present responsibilities. Do they *prevent* you or do they *allow* you to make this change? God is not the author of confusion. The Holy Spirit will give you direction.

"Howbeit when He, the Spirit of truth, is come, He will guide you into all truth" (John 16:13).

Be Prepared

It was a challenging message that the pastor gave that Sunday night. And when he extended the invitation, a number of young people responded to a call for total dedication to Christ. Later I talked with them about the preparation necessary for various callings. We discussed the fact that in most cases, they would need from one to eight years of training beyond high school.

"What?" some of them exclaimed.

This is one reason why many "would-be" followers of Christ fall by the wayside — why they never find God's will for their lives. They haven't counted the cost. They aren't willing to take the training necessary to enter the fields of service into which God has called them.

For example, if God calls you to be a Christian educator, you will need at least four years of college and perhaps more. On the other hand, if God calls you into secretarial work, you may need only one year of specialized training beyond high school. But in whatever capacity you serve the Lord, nothing will stand you in better stead than a year or two of intensive Bible training.

This I believe: There is *no* substitute for preparation. You can have all the talent in the world but if you do not have adequate training you will never be at your best. And today, technical preparation is especially important. It offers the key to many influential doors. Training? Yes! Can you imagine a fellow volunteering for the paratroopers and yet being unwilling to take the training that goes with it? When God calls a person to a specific work, He also calls him to adequate preparation. And there are always opportunities for the man who is prepared.

Have you ever thought about this? God can only use what you offer Him. If you have fingers that cannot type or play a musical instrument, God cannot

171

use you as a secretary or an organist. If your mind and tongue have not been trained in languages, God cannot use you as a translator. If you have not had training and experience in leadership, God cannot use you as a leader. In other words, limited preparedness restricts your place and field of service!

There are many Christian men and women whom God would have called into other types of work, if they had had proper training. But since they did not, God has had to use them in a less effective place. And after a certain time in life, it is almost impossible to retrace one's steps and take additional instruction. The best time for formal training is when one is young, and preferably before he is married.

So don't make the mistakes that others have made. Get all the training you can *now,* before you begin your life's work or get too involved with responsibilities. Remember, time spent in preparation is time well spent. You must live for a lifetime with the preparation you get when you're young. So develop your abilities. You'll not only be more useful to the Lord but you'll be a happier, finer person. Remember, you're *young only once!*

What Kind of Service?

If you truly want the will of God for your life it means that you are willing to do *any* kind of service into which He may lead you.

Your place may not be glamorous or where you receive acclaim. It may be a humble one — but that doesn't lessen its importance. And remember—God's values are vastly different from ours: *He has no unimportant jobs!*

The late Dr. Keith L. Brooks, whose great influence in writing has been felt around the world, used to tell of a friend who lived near his home in California. She was a physically handicapped lady who had an important ministry of intercessory prayer. Throughout each day she talked and communed with the Lord.

Dr. Brooks said that often when special requests came in the mail from various parts of the world, he took them over to this dear lady. Immediately she would start to pray. And he said that it was not at all unusual for the answers to come within a day or two; sometimes even within a few hours. Dr. Brooks told me that undoubtedly she was just as valuable to his organization as anyone he had on the payroll.

Perhaps God is calling you to such a work—one of power, but a service almost unknown to men. You may not be a great evangelist like Billy Graham. But perhaps you can be a Christian secretary. A girl in an office typing and witnessing for Christ, can fill just as important a part in the sight of God as an evangelist. Remember, *all dedicated service is sacred.* God puts no premiums on acclaim or popularity. His presence and guidance can be yours whether you serve Him in the limelight or in your "small corner." "And the Lord shall guide thee continually . . . and thou shalt be like a watered garden and like a spring of water, whose waters fail not" (Isa. 58:11).

When you consider God's will for your life, keep in mind that many times God gives a person certain responsibilities so that he will be prepared to do greater things later on. I know of a talented young minister whom God led into a small church in a little community. There he worked intimately with the people. He learned many important lessons. And a few years later God called him to a challenging pastorate in a large city.

He told me, "I would never have been prepared for this work if God had not given me several years in a small, hard community. It was the best preparation I could have had."

So, you see, it isn't the *kind* of work that is important but it is your *devotion* to God in whatever He asks you to do.

But whatever you do, don't be afraid to try *big things* for God. You have a great God with a great

173

plan—and you are part of it. Don't let your vision be hampered by fear of your own inadequacies. Remember, if you are in God's will it's *His* job you are doing —and He is able to perform it. Yes, even through you.

God makes no mistakes. Does it seem that He is asking you to do the impossible? Perhaps you have forgotten that you are in partnership with Him and that ". . . with God, all things are possible" (Matt. 19:26).

Many people can succeed in more than one kind of service; some in many different kinds. God may issue you an emergency call in some field you never dreamed of. But if God is in it, you'll be successful. Moses shrank from the task of leading the Israelites because of his own inadequacy of speech. But God used him in spite of it and made him one of the greatest leaders ever known in history.

So trust God and believe Him. When He calls you into a field of service, step out in faith and *lean hard on God*. The Bible says, "Trust in the LORD with all thine heart; and lean not unto thine own understanding. In all thy ways acknowledge him, and he shall direct thy paths" (Prov. 3:5, 6).

Direct our paths? Yes, into fruitful service for Him. This is the road to victory and accomplishment for God. And like the apostle Paul we, too, can say "I can do *all* things through Christ which strengtheneth me" (Phil. 4:13).

> In the center of the circle
>   Of the will of God I stand:
> There can come no second causes,
>   All must come from His dear hand.
> All is well! For 'tis my Father
>   Who my life hath planned. —*Author unknown*

Hindrances

Just recently a friend asked, "What do you think are the greatest hindrances that people encounter in seeking the will of God for their lives?"

174

I thought for a moment, then suggested that these were some of the greatest stumbling blocks:

(1) *Refusing to give up something that stands between them and God.*

So often young people do not find God's will for them because they have something in their lives they are not willing to give up. It might be a worldly amusement or some other seemingly little thing. But nothing is small that keeps a person from being in the center of God's will.

A man once captured a baby eagle and put him into a cage. He grew and grew until he became a large bird. But because of his confinement he had never developed his wings, so he could not fly high as God had intended him to do. One day the door of the cage was accidentally left open and the eagle escaped. He flew to a nearby tree where he roosted on a low branch. It was not long until he met an untimely death by the gun of a hunter.

This eagle missed out on God's intention for him. He was created to live in high places and to soar aloft through the sky. But because he had been captured he was doomed to live on the ground and to meet an early death.

Like the eagle, God has created you and me to live on a high spiritual plane and to carry out the great plans He has for our lives. May we yield completely to Him so that we may not be taken captive by the forces of sin which would cause us to miss His best for our lives.

(2) *Unwillingness to leave home.*

It is only natural that young people who come from happy homes should be strongly attached to their families. But when it means that God takes second place in their lives—that is wrong. We read in the Scriptures that a Christian's foes may be those of his own household. This sounds like a cruel accusation; but when a person's family keeps him from attaining God's best for his life, they are no better than enemies.

175

We can never get a vision of what God would have us do until we are willing to follow God completely—putting Him *first* in our lives.

(3) *Refusing to give up a special friend.*

Sometimes a boy friend or a girl friend can keep a person from finding God's will for his life. What a tragedy! God demands first place in a person's heart. Then He will give that person His best. It is the only road to true happiness and contentment.

(4) *Receiving advice from the wrong people.*

People who do not know Christ or who are not spiritually mature cannot give reliable advice about being in the center of God's will. You don't go to the dentist to find out what's wrong with your car. You go to someone who's an automobile mechanic.

The same holds true with regard to spiritual advice. I know a Christian young man whose music teacher encouraged him to train for light opera. Why didn't the teacher suggest gospel music? Surely there is no greater calling than singing the gospel of the Lord Jesus Christ! But the teacher had no spiritual discernment.

So choose carefully when you are seeking advice. Then check the suggestions with God's Word. And be on your guard; Satan traps many fine young people through this subtle means. Don't let him trap you!

God says, "Blessed is the man that walketh not in the *counsel* of the ungodly" (Ps. 1:1). He also tells us, "If any of you lack wisdom, let him ask of God . . ." (James 1:5).

Without a Doubt

Can you know for sure when you *are* in the center of God's will?

Yes, you can! And here are a few indications that may help you to know. First of all, you will have peace of mind. You may have troubles all around you and you may be in a difficult spot. There may be uncertainties about many things—but *you will have peace*

176

of mind. "Thou wilt keep him in perfect peace, whose mind is stayed on thee: because he trusteth in thee" (Isa. 26:3).

Another indication of being in God's will is a feeling of *satisfaction.* When you are in God's will you may not have all that you might like to have—and you may not be doing the thing that gives you popularity— but you *will* have a sense of satisfaction. It comes from realizing that you are doing what God would have you do.

Have you ever noticed that people who are in God's will are happy? This doesn't mean that they are exempt from difficulties. But because they have Christ in their hearts and because they are obeying God, they have joy. What does it take to make a person happy? For someone who is unsaved, a measure of happiness comes from doing what he likes to do. But with a Christian, happiness comes from *doing the will of God.* When you are doing what He would have you do, He will fill your life with joy and happiness.

When you are in the center of God's will you will be a *blessing to others.* You will not hinder them and you will not be in competition with them. You will be an inspiration even though there may be some around you who do not know Christ or who may dislike the fact that you are serving the Lord. Whether you are working in an office, teaching school, or serving on a foreign field, you will be a blessing to others if you are in God's will. This is a mark of a fruitful Christian. You are not pleasing yourself; but you are pleasing God and He is using you.

Here's a good rule to remember: When you are in the will of God you will not be in conflict with the teachings of the Bible. A person cannot possibly be in the center of God's will and still be doing something that is definitely contrary to the teachings of His Word. So if your activities don't agree with what the Bible teaches, then you are out of God's will.

Continuing in His Will

"The secret of success is constancy to purpose."

This is true in our Christian life. To be used of God we must *continue* to follow Him and not get side tracked. And of course Satan is busy trying to derail Christians.

The Bible gives us the fascinating account of the prophet Jonah. God told him to go to Nineveh. But did he do it? No. Instead he boarded a ship going in the opposite direction. He didn't *want* to follow God. But God wasn't going to let His servant get away with this. So the Lord sent a terrible storm—so violent that the crew and all the passengers of the ship feared for their lives. Then Jonah confessed that *he* was the cause of the storm. So they threw him overboard and immediately the waters were calm.

But God had His hand on Jonah and he did not die. God had prepared a great fish to swallow him and to carry him to dry land. After three days and three nights the fish disgorged him.

What a horrible experience! What a hard lesson to learn! But after that, Jonah went to Nineveh. And of course when he went where God wanted him, God blessed him.

Jonah was *in* God's will at first but then he got *out* of God's will; then finally he was back *in* God's will again. Jonah was punished when he was *out* of God's will—it was necessary that he might learn a lesson of obedience. God warns us that "As many as I love I rebuke and chasten: Be zealous therefore, and repent" (Rev. 3:19).

How then, does a person stay in the center of God's will? Simply by doing the very things that originally led him into finding God's will.

At the conclusion of a youth meeting, a girl asked the speaker this startling question: "How can I be a Christian and still have my own way?" Perhaps we may never have put it in so many words but we may have consciously or unconsciously wondered as much. We have sought, in a measure at least, to do God's will but we have reserved the right to have our way whenever possible. This is not God's plan. Our Christian life and service for Him *must* be dedicated without reservation if we are to be happy and effective. God says, "For my thoughts are not your thoughts, neither are your ways my ways, saith the LORD" (Isa. 55:8).

I think of Phil. He had lots of ability and personality. And when he graduated from Bible college he felt sure that God had called him into the ministry. But he decided to take a job for a year or so before going on to seminary. Phil's personality and natural talent served him well and it wasn't long before he had a good job with a much higher salary than he would receive as a minister. After a short time he decided that he just wasn't "cut out" for the ministry. He reasoned this way: "I can honor God just as much by being a business man." Friends were puzzled. They did not know whether he was *in* or *out* of God's will. But a year or so later they knew! Why? Because he had lost his joy, he was restless and unsettled—and he was not even found in God's house on Sundays. Phil didn't witness anymore. Oh yes, he made money. But it did not bring him satisfaction.

Of course God *could* have been calling Phil into a new field of service. He sometimes does. But in this case it was apparent that Phil was out of God's will.

So let's keep on our toes. Just because a person has once been in God's will doesn't mean he automatically stays there. It's something we must keep working at—and keep praying for. It has been well stated that "if what you did yesterday still looks big, then you have done nothing today."

Perhaps you need to stop and ask yourself, "Am I *still* in God's will? Are the coals of my spiritual fire still burning or are they the ashes of yesterday?"

179

The Blueprints

A distinguished engineer was confined to his bed for awhile. But because of his reputation and unusual skill he was asked to draw the blueprints for a great suspension bridge. In due time the detailed plans were completed and placed in the hands of those who were to do the work.

Months passed, and at last the bridge was finished. One day several of his friends came to the engineer's room and carried him to a place where he could view the magnificent bridge spanning the wide river. Tears filled his eyes, and looking down at the blueprints in his hands he said, "It's just like the plan!"

God also has his blueprints for every life. They have been worked out in minute detail—and they are flawless. Have you found His plan for *your* life?

Someday in eternity you will look back over your life. What a joy it will be if you can hear God say, "It's just like the plan!"